YES, I CAN SAY THAT

WHEN THEY COME FOR
THE COMEDIANS, WE
ARE ALL IN TROUBLE

JUDY GOLD

DEY ST.
An Imprint of WILLIAM MORROW

FIRST EDITION

Designed by Paula Russell Szafranski

Names: Gold, Judy, 1962– author.
Title: Yes I can say that : when they come for the comedians we're all in trouble / Judy Gold.
Description: First edition. | New York : Dey Street, 2020. | Includes bibliographical references. | Summary: "Judy Gold, a concise, funny, and thoughtful polemic on the current assault on comedy, that explores how it is undermining free speech and a fundamental attack against the integrity of the art. From Mae West and Lenny Bruce to Richard Pryor and Howard Stern to Kathy Griffith and Kevin Hart, comedians have long been under fire for using provocative, often taboo subjects to challenge mores and get a laugh. But in the age of social media, comedians are at greater risk of being silenced, enduring shaming, threats, and damaged careers because of angry, censorious electronic mobs. But while comedians' work has often been used to rile up detractors, a new threat has emerged from the left: identity politics and notions like "safetyism" and trigger warnings that are now creating a cultural and political standard that runs perilously close to censorship. From college campuses to the Oscars, comics are being censured for old jokes, long-standing comedy traditions, unfinished bits and old material that instead of being forgotten, go viral. For comics like Judy Gold, today's attacks on comics would have Richard Pryor and Lenny Bruce "rolling in their graves." "No one has the right to tell comics what they can or cannot joke about. Do you tell artists what they can or cannot paint?" she asks. Freedom of speech is fundamental for great stand-up comedy. Humor is the most palatable way to discuss a subversive or taboo topic, but it better be funny. A comic's observations are deliberately delivered to entertain, provoke, and lead to an exchange of ideas. "We are truth tellers." More important, the tolerance of free speech is essential for a healthy democracy. In addition to offering readers a quick study on the history of comedy and the arts (noting such historical reference points as The Hays Code) and the threats to them., Gold takes readers on a hilarious ride with chapters such as "Thank God Don Rickles is Dead," as well as her singular take on "micro-aggressions," such as: Person: "OMG! You're a lesbian? I had no idea. I mean you wear make-up. When did you become a lesbian?" Judy Gold: "Coincidently, right after I met you!" (micro-assault!) In this era of "fake news," partisan politics, and heated rhetoric, the need to protect free speech has never been greater, especially for comics, who often serve as the canaries in the coalmine, monitoring the health of our democracy. Yes I Can Say That is a funny and provocative look at how safe spaces are the very antithesis of comedy as an art form-and an urgent call to arms to protect our most fundamental Constitutional right. There's a good reason it was the FIRST amendment"—Provided by publisher.
Identifiers: LCCN 2019054781 | ISBN 9780062953759 (hardcover) | ISBN 9780062953773 (ebook)
Subjects: LCSH: Comedy—Political aspects—United States. | Censorship—United States. | Freedom of speech—United States. | Political correctness—United States.
Classification: LCC PN1929.P65 G65 2020 | DDC 792.7/6—dc23
LC record available at https://lccn.loc.gov/2019054781

ISBN 978-0-06-295375-9

20 21 22 23 24   LSC   10 9 8 7 6 5 4 3 2 1

YES, I CAN
SAY THAT

In memory of "Uncle" Bob Smith, whose
reverence for language was unparalleled;
whose unrepentant honesty, dignity, and pride
in being gay was intoxicating; and whose
hilarious comedy changed the conversation.
Thank you for filling our lives with love and laughter.
We miss you every second of every day.

And to all of the comedians on stages all over
the world, who every single night fearlessly
tell their stories, speak truth to power,
and make the world laugh.

CONTENTS

FOREWORD

Judy, why are you writing the foreword to your own book? Because I hate asking people for favors unless it includes some type of massage.

Since our beginning, human beings have instinctively known that laughing is good for you. The saying "laughter is the best medicine" is derived from the book of Proverbs. And, despite the passage of thousands of years, people today are pretty much laughing at the same things our ancestors were laughing at in biblical times—each other, ourselves, our differences, and the flickers of recognition that confirm we're all the same. Good jokes are infused with human emotions accessible to everyone.

When I was approached to write a book on the freedom of speech from a comedian's perspective, I was elated that someone at a large publishing house thought that my point of view on the topic warranted enough interest to write a book. But, the more I wrote, the more I realized that there was no way to fit in everything and everyone. The list of comedians, actors, satirists, cartoonists, journalists, writers, and other artists whose work exemplifies the sacredness of our First Amendment rights is far too long for me to pay homage to them individually. Suffice it to say, I believe we are all blessed by those who paved the way and broke down barriers so we could laugh while speaking truth to power.

My viewpoints and opinions are based on my almost four decades of experience as a comedian. I performed my first stand-up set in 1981, and from that point on, I was hooked. I have been far from perfect with my use of language, and I, like most comics, regret bits or jokes I've done that went too far. In the 1980s, comics working in comedy clubs could basically say whatever they wanted. No subject was taboo, but the key was—and still is—that if you were going to joke about a subversive topic, like race, religion, sex, politics, or death, it had to be funny. Some people would laugh. Some people wouldn't. Some would applaud. Some wouldn't. Then they'd pay their two-drink minimum, and we'd all go home and move on with our lives.

Several months ago, one of my favorite comedians, Dave Attell, asked me if I thought he could include a joke in one of his specials without backlash. Dave is arguably one of the funniest, quickest, most fearless, and most politically incorrect comics working today. I couldn't believe that even *he* was worrying about possible retaliation for one of his hilarious bits. It's terrifying out there right now for stand-ups.

My goal was to write a book that not only makes people think but sparks conversation. As you make your way through these pages, I hope you gain some understanding of what it's like to be a comedian in 2020. I sincerely want you to develop an appreciation of the role comedy plays in fostering healing and cohesion during difficult periods like the present, when our fragile democracy is under attack. But most of all, no matter what, I want you to keep laughing.

Eternity is a mere moment,
just long enough for a joke.

—HERMANN HESSE

1

It's Not Funny Until the Fat Lady Cries

Going to a comedy club and
expecting not to get offended is
like going on a roller coaster and
expecting not to get scared.

—EDDIE SARFATY

I've never cried in front of my therapist, and believe me, I've had lots and lots of therapists, and even more reasons to cry. I always felt that if I shed tears in a therapy session, the therapists would have all the power. Naturally, I felt like they were trying to make me cry, as if they were manipulating me in some way. If I gave in to their manipulation, it would be a sign of weakness. My parents had taught my siblings and me that when people show their emotions, especially in public, it's because they want attention. It's fake. And so everyone in my immediate family suffered in silence. I remember when I was six years old, my brother, sister, and I were watching *Rudolph the Red-Nosed Reindeer* upstairs on my parents' black-and-white television. Near the end of the movie, when Santa promises to find loving homes for all the misfit toys and announces that Christmas isn't canceled after all because Rudolph's bright red nose is going to lead the sleigh through the storm, I started crying. Hysterically bawling. All those misfits who'd been shunned and mocked were finally vindicated. I put my hands on either side of my head like horse blinders so my siblings couldn't see my tears, but of course, they knew exactly what was happening, especially with the sniffling sounds and quick staccato breaths. That was their cue to berate me and tease me for crying over a fake reindeer. I was the youngest, and humiliating me was their job. I was mortified—well, as much as a six-year-old is capable of being mortified. They caught me at my most vulnerable moment and laughed at me. That would be the first of thousands of times I would be made fun of for something out of my control. That's one of the major factors in why I became a stand-up comedian.

Another reason I chose a profession where the goal is to elicit laughter on your own terms is that by the time I was thirteen years old, I was already six feet tall. Being an uncoordinated six-foot-tall eighth grader was not what every adolescent Jewish girl in New Jersey dreamed of in 1975. I was taller than my mother, my older sister, my teachers, the principal, my parents' friends, my friends' parents, and the rabbi presiding over my bat mitzvah. I would grow three more inches (only to later lose one of them to knee replacement surgery), join my school's marching band, and endure days filled with kids yelling "Bigfoot," "Sasquatch," "Orca," "Jolly Green Giant," or "Big Bird" every time I walked down the hallway. I rarely told my mother what was happening at school because the last time she took me to the doctor to get measured and weighed, the two of them sat there, for what seemed like forever, telling me how lucky I was to be so tall. After the pump-Judith-up session, my mother asked me to leave the room for a minute so she could talk to the doctor alone. With my ear pressed against the other side of the door, I heard my mother say, "WHEN IS IT GOING TO STOP?" That's when I learned that most people are full of shit. Oh, and that was also my first joke.

Whenever I did break down and tell my mother about the abuse I was dealing with at school, her only advice was to ignore it. She would tell me that the kids were picking on me because they were little pipsqueaks who were jealous of my height and that all of them secretly wished they were as tall as me. I wore a size 12 shoe by the time I was twelve years old, so when my teachers would recite that old maxim "Act your age, not your shoe size," I would reply, "Same thing." I took my mother's advice to heart, and even though I heard every single taunt loud and clear, you would never have known by looking at me. I simply acted as if I'd heard nothing or that I was preoccupied with something else. Since there were no cell phones, I couldn't fake that I was texting or on a call. I had to be creative. I'd pretend I was looking for something in my bag, start a conversation with a person nearby, or act like I forgot something and walk in the opposite direction. My last therapist, who happens to have the same name as my mother (Mommy), told me that my real Mommy gave me the wrong advice—I should have stuck up for myself, one-upped them with a slight, and shut them the fuck up. She was right. I had dozens of retorts waiting inside my head, but the problem was, that's exactly where they stayed—inside my head.

The few people I hung out with knew I was funny, and in fact, in my small group of misfit toys, I was Rudolph. I led the way. I made the jokes and my friends laughed. It was awesome! Finally, people were laughing *with* me rather than *at* me. I was controlling what they were laughing about. It was the greatest feeling in the world. Who needed to compete with those popular kids, anyway? I was perfectly fine with the other misfits, and in reality, there were plenty of other oddballs who made me look like Jaclyn Smith (a.k.a. Kelly Garrett on *Charlie's Angels*) in comparison. So, I looked at the bright side—except when I would focus on my sexuality. That was a secret I hung on to like my life depended on it. At that time, it did.

You might be thinking that you've heard some version of this story before. It seems that any time a performer or writer who doesn't fit the Hollywood mold wins an Emmy, Tony, Oscar, or Grammy, they dedicate their award to all those other people out there who are in the midst of the same struggles they had to endure themselves. The battles of being in show biz sans famous or powerful relatives are hard enough. Fighting your way as someone who's homeless, disabled, overweight (except if you're male), over-tall (except if you're male), a little person, a person of color, someone on death's door—I could go on and on and on—makes everything so much more difficult. It also does something else. It gives you thick skin. It teaches you how to stick up for yourself. And it gives you a choice—to feel angry or offended, or to find the funny and not take yourself so seriously. I truly believe that the more humiliation and torment you experienced in your formative years, the more likely you are to have a wicked sense of humor. There's nothing better than a good laugh . . . okay, maybe one other thing, but that gets way more difficult to achieve when you get older.

Comedy is the most palatable way to acknowledge the universality of our idiosyncrasies, eccentricities, and shortcomings. When you break it down, we're all just human beings doing the best we can. Think about the last time you shared a big laugh with someone you're really close to. Did you laugh at something only the two of you would get? Was it something mean about someone else? Did you have to be there? And if you answered yes to any or all of those questions, was it naughty? The best comedy lives on the edge of what's acceptable. Jokes are nourished by tension; laughter is a release. Sharing laughs with others creates a sort of nonthreatening intimacy that increases our identification with one another. When you laugh with someone, any differences you have with that person seem to fade away for a few moments. Laughter brings people together, but lately it seems like a lot of people are making the choice to be outraged by a single word, term, or thought rather than considering the context or a speaker's intent. This is a result of political correctness (an expression

I've come to abhor) run amok, with both old and new jargon taking on lives of their own.

Once a year, new words or expressions are chosen to be added to the dictionary and therefore forever validated in our lexicons. (In fact, in 2014, I was honored to be asked to make a video announcing that the Yiddish word *schmutz* had been added to the *Merriam-Webster's Official Scrabble Players Dictionary*.) In the early 1960s, when I was born, some of those new words were *carpool, fender bender, junk food, reality check, trendsetting, toaster oven, diddly-squat, skinny-dip, degradable, miniskirt, zip code,* and *sleepover*. This should give you a sense of what was going on during that time.

The term *politically correct* was first used in 1793 to mean exactly what it sounds like—the correct thing to say or do politically. In the 1970s, folks on the left often used the term in a satirical, self-critical way, such as when feminists mocked the conflicts between the real across-the-board equality they were fighting for and the romanticized second-class expectations of marriage and motherhood with which they'd been inculcated. "I'd love to burn my bra with you ladies, but my husband married me for my perky breasts." It wasn't until the late twentieth century when conservatives weaponized the term. They attacked progressives' efforts to use *political correctness* to eliminate language insulting to specific groups and expand the use of the autonyms those groups had chosen for themselves. The word *microaggression* was included in the 1970 edition of the dictionary after it was coined by psychiatrist Chester M. Pierce. Per the *Merriam-Webster Dictionary*, a microaggression is "A comment or action that subtly and often unconsciously or unintentionally expresses a prejudiced attitude toward a member of a marginalized group (such as a racial minority)." More recently, however, *microaggression* has been expanded to include pretty much any word or action that makes someone—regardless of whether they are marginalized—feel insulted, invisible, or uncomfortable. They are minuscule slights, subtle hostilities, and snubs that have nothing to do with a person's immutable characteristics. Basically, they are excuses for crybabies to make mountains out of molehills in an attempt to justify their persecution complexes. Microaggressions can apparently lead to "microtraumas." Are you scared yet? If you are, perhaps you should call a "microtherapist," join a "microsupport group," or maybe get a "micro-emotional-support animal."

Microaggressions seem to occur in three forms: microassault, microinvalidation, and microinsult.[1] Here are some examples of microaggressions I've experienced for being Jewish, being a lesbian, and being six foot two. This is where a sense of humor comes in handy.

OMG! You're a lesbian? I had no idea. I mean, you wear makeup.
   When did you become a lesbian?
Coincidently, right after I met you!
....
#microassault

You just haven't met the right guy. I could turn you.
Yeah, you could turn me into a bigger lesbian.
....
#microinvalidation

Your son is even taller than you. Thank God he's a boy!
I KNOW!! Otherwise he would end up miserable, barren, and
   alone—just like me.
....
#microinsult

Are you planning on raising your children as homosexuals?

Actually, yes! They're only allowed to listen to show tunes, and we don't have any bedrooms in our apartment, so they'll be living in the closet for the first eighteen years of their lives.

#microstupidfuckingquestion

You're Jewish, right?

No, my last name is Gold. I use a diffuser on my blow-dryer. And I spoke to my mother on the phone multiple times a day when she was alive. Do you think this spot on my arm is cancer?

#microimbecile

Wait. Do Jews celebrate Thanksgiving?

Yes, we do. They just granted us full US holiday celebratory rights.

#microfuckingignorant

Wait a minute! What do you mean, they have two moms? How is that possible? Who's the real mother?

We forgot.

#microlivingunderarock

Mental health professionals claim that microaggressions can lead to anxiety, depression, and poor health. DUH! Why do you think so many Jews are in therapy? Because Jewish mothers are expert microaggressors. Let me give you an example of my own mother's expertise at this.

MOM: Hello?

JUDY: Hi, Mom. I wanted to let you know that I'll be on *The View* tomorrow.

MOM: Oh, very nice. I'll watch. What's the topic this time?

JUDY: It's Pride week, so I'm talking about being a lesbian mom.

MOM: They must have a lot of airtime to fill. (*microaggression*)

JUDY: What's that supposed to mean?

MOM: [*pause*] I'm very dizzy right now, Judith. I'll have to call you later. (*Jewish-guilt aggression*)

So, let's analyze what happened here. I was excited to share something with my mother that I thought would fill her with pride (pun intended). Why I thought that could be even a remote possibility is an entirely different issue. Instead of responding to me with a statement of support, she pulled her usual "avoid the topic" trick of telling me she's dizzy or that she doesn't feel well. This way, I'm not only disappointed, but I get the bonus of feeling guilty as well! Could this be an example of why I suffer from anxiety, depression, and self-doubt? Absolutely! Is that her fault? Probably. But who cares? She gave me tough skin, a great sense of humor, and years of stand-up material.

According to the new, broader application of the term microaggression, I, as a stand-up comedian, am constantly subjected to them. For some reason, if you're not a household name, people think your livelihood is just a hobby.

Oh, you do stand-up comedy? Have I seen you on anything?
Yes, your wife.

How come you're not on *Saturday Night Live*?
Great question! I filled out the application, and I'm just waiting to hear back. Fingers crossed!

You're a comedian. Say something funny.
You're an accountant. Do my taxes.

For a female, you're pretty funny.
For an asshole, you're pretty clean.

Of course, by their very nature, comedians know that the best way to handle serial microaggressors is to one-up them with a clever slight—something most people subjected to micro-aggressions aren't skilled in. That said, comedy doesn't always work because sometimes old words suddenly have new meanings and connotations that make things trickier. For example, in the wrong context, formerly innocuous words like *woke*, *snowflake*, and *deplorable* can stir up emotions like never before. The ever-increasing and -changing stakes placed on individual words is detrimental to comedy and can be very destructive for the performer and writer as well.

In May 2018, Ivanka Trump shared a photo on Twitter of herself holding her baby son with the caption "I♥! #SundayMorning." She posted this photo in the midst of news stories about migrant children arriving in the US and not only being separated from their parents but also being held in cages without basic human necessities. That anyone, due to privilege, could be so blind and deaf to the suffering of others is disheartening. For the woman supposedly serving as the administration's advocate for the families and children suffering because of these reprehensible policies to post something so oblivious is simply horrendous. Her photo and caption clearly fit the definition of a microaggression, albeit (hopefully) an unintentional one.

In response, Samantha Bee, the creator and host of the TBS show *Full Frontal with Samantha Bee,* chided President Trump's daughter and advisor for posting something so insensitive and, in the process, referred to Ivanka as a "feckless cunt." Prior to this incident, Bee had used the C-word many times on her show without controversy. She has always wanted to take the word back from the misogynists and empower it. I'm 100 percent with her on this. But perhaps using *cunt* as an insult wasn't the best decision. She was name-calling, and that, instead of the real issue at hand—the obvious thoughtlessness of the First Daughter's post—became the focus of the controversy.

The Orange Leader of the Free World called for Bee to be fired. Yes, the very same guy who was recorded saying that he likes to grab women by the pussy, who has called women "fat pigs," "dogs," "horse-faced," and "low IQ," and who's been accused of intentionally barging in on semi-naked teens competing in the Miss Teen USA contest called for a comedian to be fired for insulting his daughter. Give me a fucking break.

Bee did issue an apology, but it wasn't the one Trump and his supporters wanted. She simply apologized for using the word *cunt* as an insult. She apologized to women who had been called "cunts" at the worst moments of their lives and who wished they never had to hear that word again. She talked about how this controversy created a distraction from the real issues. This is what happens when you focus on individual words without considering context. At the end of her apology, Bee said:

> I would do anything to help those kids. I hate that this distracted from them, so to them, I am also sorry. And look, if you are worried about the death of civility, don't sweat it. I'm a comedian. People who hone their voices in basement bars while yelling back at drunk hecklers are definitely not paragons of civility. I am, I'm really sorry that

I said that word, but you know what? Civility is just nice words. Maybe we should all worry a little bit more about the niceness of our actions.

When you take a moment to truly understand the intent of the joke and the joke teller, it leaves you with a lot more than a laugh. In pointing out the matter-of-fact benefits afforded to—and expected by—those who are rich, white, and beautiful (and, in Ivanka's case, have access to real political power), Bee was asking us to think, to question the status quo. By making fun of Ivanka's cluelessness and drawing out our laughter, Bee enlisted us in condemning the microaggression inherent in the myopic tweet.

Some things are microaggressions; some things aren't. Ivanka's statement, a subtle and probably unintentional slight of desperate immigrant families, is. Samantha Bee's name-calling is not. Immigrants are marginalized. Ivanka is more than privileged, and she needs no protection from feeling hurt or left out. And if she's sad, she could purchase something—or someone—to make her feel better. I learned at the age of six that that's not how real life works. So why don't you do yourself a favor and take a deep breath, relax, pour yourself a microbrew, and stop taking yourself so fucking seriously.

2

Say That Again, and I'll Wash Your Mouth Out with Soap

Judith, why do you have to curse
so much onstage? Do you really
need to use that vocabulary?
Bill Cosby never curses in his act.

—RUTH GOLD, 2007

started using bad words at a very young age. It's a Jersey thing. My parents only cursed when they were really pissed off. Some of their greatest hits included "up shit's creek without a paddle," "goddamn son of a bitch," "bitch on wheels," "oh shit," and "goddamn it, Judith!!!" I never heard them say the word *fuck*. And like most kids of my generation, I thought they were the only parents who ever used bad language. That all ended when I was in first grade.

On Yom Kippur, one of the holiest days in the Jewish calendar, Jews sit in synagogue all day and ask God to forgive them for all the horrible things they've done in the past year. We do this while fasting for up to twenty-five hours. Children are not required to fast until they have had their bar or bat mitzvah. Up until I was thirteen, my mother would take me home during the afternoon break and make me a peanut butter sandwich (peanut butter was our friend back then—nobody went into anaphylaxis), and then we'd go right back to services. I was always so damn hungry when we got home that I would shove the sandwich down my throat in thirty seconds and then quickly drink a glass of milk to wash it down. One particular Yom Kippur, when I was six years old, my mother and I did our annual routine. When we got back to the synagogue, I was sitting on my mother's lap in the pews.

Services began and I whispered to her, "Mommy, I feel sick." She told me it was because I ate too fast. "But I feel *really* sick." She told me it would go away in a few minutes. "No, it's really bad. I need to go to the bathroom." And just as she took me off her lap and we stood up to go to the bathroom, I projectile vomited all over the sanctuary. My mother quickly grabbed me and brought me outside to get some air. She sat me down on the steps leading up to the building's entrance. Herb, the maintenance guy/Shabbos goy, was there, too. All of a sudden, one of the big machers walks outside with his ten-foot-long tallit around his shoulders and says to Herb, "You've got to do something. It smells like shit in there." I was shocked that this pious man, wearing a yarmulke and a prayer shawl, just said "shit." I thought my parents were the only ones who said those bad words, and that was the reason they were asking God for forgiveness. The most interesting thing was that it made me dislike Mr. Big Macher. I thought he was a jerk for completely disregarding my feelings and using that language in front of me. Every time I saw him after that, I wanted to tell him that he smelled like shit. He triggered me, but eventually I got over it.

The word *trigger* used to be reserved for therapists to help patients identify and avoid particular stimuli that brought up past traumas or caused certain reactions. It was also used to explain the behavior of people with autism. Now, however, the term has been hijacked by delicate flowers who use it to describe words, actions, or events that cause them even the slightest bit of unpleasantness. *Trigger* has spun out of control and no longer serves its original purpose of protecting those who actually need it. Remember when people ignored little things that made them uncomfortable or just let them roll off their back? Those days are long gone. No more of that. Our society is at the point where feeling uncomfortable is so completely unacceptable that people play the "trigger" card to silence different views and opinions. This stifles comedians more than any other group. This thought process has resulted, and continues to result, in the banning of words, topics, and ideas that cause people to feel uneasy.

According to the United Nations' 2018 *World Population Prospects* report, a baby is born in the United States approximately every eight seconds, and I'll bet you that someone in this country is triggered more often than that. We have trigger words, trigger posts, trigger sounds, trigger sights, trigger songs, trigger smells, trigger foods, trigger sensations, and on and on, ad nauseam. The longer you live, the more connections you have to things, so obviously the more triggers you have. And if you happen to be easily triggered, exactly whose fault is that? The unknowing comedian? Is it the comedian's job to anticipate every possible joke or word that might trigger an individual audience member? No fucking way. It's getting to the point where if I make a joke about my friend's three-year-old dog, and someone in the audience's three-year-old dog was recently hit by a car, that person feels that they have the right to chastise me, either in person during or after the show, or on a social media platform. Guess what, folks? The world doesn't revolve around you.

Since the first jokes were told, there have always been comedians who've used words and topics that have offended some people. There have always been people who, in response, have attempted to ban those words and shut down comedians and artists speaking their truth to those topics. Historically, this has primarily come from the right—people professing religious or moral reasons for prohibiting certain speech. A good illustration of this is the Hays Code.

From 1930 to 1968, films produced by major studios used the Motion Picture Production Code, also known as the Hays Code, named for Will Hays, the president of the Motion Picture Producers and Distributors of America at the time. The Hays Code was created in 1930 but started to be strictly enforced in 1934. No wonder it was called the Depression Era.

There were two parts of the code. The first was called "General Principles," and it prohibited a film from lowering the standards of those who viewed it. The second was called "Particular Applications," which listed themes and items that were prohibited from being depicted in films. (They seemed to love the word *prohibit* in those days.) Some of the prohibited items were cursing, nudity, pregnancy, the word *virgin,* premarital sex, homosexuality, bestiality, interracial relationships, kisses lasting more than three seconds, venereal disease, blasphemy, and all criminal activity. So now you know why Clark Gable never ordered a Bloody Mary.

The Hays Code also strove to censor or shut down comedians and artists because there were people in powerful positions interested in maintaining the status quo and avoiding some undesirable truths. The code stated that authority figures in films had to be depicted and treated with respect, and clergy could not be portrayed as comic characters or villains. I'm pretty sure my home movies would have been banned. I mean, these people were more controlling than my ex-girlfriend.

In the 1940s, the "Big Five" studios (Paramount, MGM, Warner Bros., 20th Century Fox, and RKO) were forced by the Supreme Court to sell their theater chains so that the smaller studios could compete fairly. The court's ruling all but stopped the Motion Picture Association of America's ability to enforce the Hays Code. (I feel like the *Law & Order* theme should sound every time I mention the code.) Then came the Hollywood blacklist of the late 1940s and '50s, when actors, writers, and directors were banned

from working because of their allegedly subversive political leanings. Why does this sound so familiar? Here is one of the many
reasons why I worship Eleanor Roosevelt:

> The film industry is a great industry with infinite pos-
> sibilities for good and bad. Its primary purpose is to en-
> tertain people. On the side, it can do many other things.
> It can popularize certain ideals, it can make education
> palatable. But in the long run, the judge who decides
> whether what it does is good or bad is the man or woman
> who attends the movies. In a democratic country I do not
> think the public will tolerate a removal of its right to de-
> cide what it thinks of the ideas and performances of those
> who make the movie industry work.[1]

In 1952 came another SCOTUS decision saying that an artistic
medium is protected under the First Amendment. Finally, in 1966,
Jack Valenti, the president of the Motion Picture Association of
America at the time, moved to a rating system that evolved over
the years into the system we presently use. In 1984, the films *Indi-
ana Jones and the Temple of Doom* and *Gremlins* were the catalysts
for the adoption of the PG-13 rating.

As we evolved, so did the morals police. The rating system
they created enabled adults to choose which films they wanted
to see for themselves and which films were appropriate for their
children to view. No one can tell a filmmaker they can't make a
film or a screenwriter they can't write a screenplay, but executives
at networks and movie studios can still decide what the public
gets to see.

The great Lenny Bruce said, "Take away the right to say
'fuck,' and you take away the right to say, 'fuck the government.'"

But it seems that it's no longer just right-wing conservatives who are silencing comedians and artists. Attempts at censorship are now coming from the so-called progressive left as well. Political correctness has somehow resulted in not just adding a dimension of discomfort to the meaning of words, but a fear of the words themselves—so much so that uttering certain words, no matter the context, cannot be tolerated, and in some instances can seriously damage a comedian's career.

Based on this new interpretation of the word *trigger*, we are all triggerers and triggerees, triggering and being triggered all day long. Who the hell has time for that? I have to finish last Sunday's *New York Times* crossword puzzle. All right, Friday's. Okay, Monday's. Go fuck yourself.

The moment my alarm goes off in the morning, I'm triggered. I'm triggered into pressing the snooze button and ridding my still half-asleep brain of self-hate. I'm triggered into wanting to throw the phone across the room when I hear, *"Please hold while our automated system helps you."* When I get to the subway and see that there's a delay, I'm triggered into cursing about how everything is so hard for me—first in a whisper and then escalating into a completely audible monologue. "Why is this happening? What did I do in a past life to deserve this? Why are you doing this to me, God? Why are you always making me late? WHY?" For extra dramatic effect, I look up at the ceiling as if God and I are having a direct conversation. I act as if this delay is something that is only happening to ME and no one else. I play the victim and reinforce how the entire world is against me. I always said that my autobiography would be titled *The Jewish Book of "Why Me?"*

My way of thinking is unhealthy, to say the least. I'm blaming the universe for purposely making my life miserable, for making me late, when in reality I just allow everyday inconveniences to take over my psyche. I take no responsibility for not leaving my apartment earlier even though I know full well that the subway is always delayed and I never give myself enough time to get anywhere. I play the victim, and when you choose to play the victim, you can pretty much blame everyone and everything else for all the bad things that happen to you. It's a really destructive and unhealthy way of thinking, believe me. I've been in therapy since 1980.

People who get automatically triggered or offended by a word or action coming from a comedian do themselves a huge disservice. It's like jurors ignoring a murderer's intent when deciding a verdict. It wouldn't matter if the murder was an accident, self-defense, mistaken identity, or done to save one person's life or many people's lives. That's it. You pulled the trigger, you're guilty. It's a lazy, close-minded, and destructive way of thinking.

Look, I'm not saying that there are no offensive words in the English language. There are plenty—and many of them can be triggers. But just because something *can* be a trigger doesn't mean it always functions as one. And in the instances where it does, it's unlikely to trigger everyone. There's a brilliant George Carlin bit that begins with a list of offensive words designed to offend as many people as possible:

> There's a different group to get pissed off at you in this country for everything you're not supposed to say. Can't say nigger, boogie, jig, jigaboo, skinhead, moolie, moulinyan, schvartze, jungle bunny. Greaser, greaseball, dago, guinea, wop, ginzo, kike, zebe, Hebe, Yid, mocky, Hymie, Mick, donkey, turkey, Limey, frog. Zip, zipperhead, squarehead, kraut, heine, Jerry, Hun, slope, slopehead, chink, gook . . .

As the lengthy bit continues, Carlin switches his tone and goes on to explain that the words in and of themselves are innocent, and that it's only the context and the speaker's intention that make them good or bad.

Things have changed since Carlin first did that routine in 1972. These days it's acknowledged—except by racists and idiots—that the N-word is offensive, disparaging, hateful, harmful, hurtful, and belittling. It's so abhorrent that it absolutely cannot be uttered by a non-black person under any circumstances—and that's why it's referred to as "the N-word." The substitution has been extended to any and every time the word is used, no matter the context. Even if someone used the word in this sentence: "N****r is a vile, inappropriate, and racist word that should never be uttered in this house again," there would be backlash.

It would behoove people to stop labeling things as "triggers" on someone else's behalf. If you're outside my purview, it's presumptuous of you to declare how I'm supposed to feel. Who the hell are you? You haven't lived my life. There are certain words I can say and certain topics I can joke about because I'm part of the communities that own them. I happen to call my friends "gay," "fags," "dykes," "bull dykes," and "queens" quite often, and they say those words right back to me. My agent, whom I refer to as my "gay-gent," is a retired chorus boy. He posts a lot of photos of himself and his husband on social media. My comment on most of his posts, whether the two of them are all dressed up just to watch the Academy Awards on TV or they're hiking and fawning over a beautiful flower or they're just being annoyingly happy, is "GAY!" That's it. They know it's my way of saying, "I love you." I have the freedom to say whatever I want because they're well aware of where it's coming from. It might be a slur to you, but it's a term of endearment between us.

I can also do Jewish jokes—and that includes Holocaust jokes. I'm a Jew. But can other people do jokes about Jews? It depends on what the joke is and who's telling it. Jokes about other races or types of people can be acceptable when they're coming from a place of knowledge, thoughtfulness, and respect. In our efforts to protect any group that's not white, Christian, straight, and male from being offended (and to prevent ourselves from being labeled as racist, homophobic, anti-Semitic, and misogynist assholes), people have begun to allow themselves to get triggered any time a marginalized person or group is even mentioned in a comedy bit. Who the fuck are we protecting by forbidding words and ideas? This school of thought is popular with most college bookers today, and it's why more and more comedians are refusing to perform at colleges and universities.

Take, for example, Nimesh Patel. Nimesh is a hilarious comedian who happens to have been the first Indian American writer for *Saturday Night Live*. He was booked at Columbia University in New York City—a college known as one of our country's bastions of education and free thought. Boy, have times changed. Nimesh never got the chance to finish his show at Columbia because his mic was cut off fairly early in his set and he was asked to leave. Here's the bit that got him in trouble:

I live in Hell's Kitchen, a diverse area in New York populated by, among others, gay black men who are not shy about telling me they don't approve of what I'm wearing. I try to learn things from everyone I encounter, and one day I realize, oh, this is how you know being gay can't be a choice—no one would choose to be gay if they're already black. No one is doubling down on hardship....No black

dude wakes up and thinks that being a black man in
America is too easy. No black dude says, "I'm going to put
on a Madonna halter top and some Jordans and make an
Indian dude real uncomfortable." That's not a choice.

What Nimesh is saying, in a very funny and provocative way,
is that being gay is especially hard for people of color, who are
already struggling against systemic racism.

For years and years, my community has had to shove this bit
of truth down the throats of people who believe that being gay
is a choice. Why would anyone *choose* to live as a second-class
citizen? Especially if you're already treated as one? Growing up
in a homophobic environment is a sad reality for many gay people
of color, and the shame they live with for being gay can be im-
measurable. While people of color usually can't hide their black-
ness or brownness, they *can* hide their sexual orientation. Nimesh
wrote a joke validating the fact that sexuality is not a choice. The
choices for the audience and the show's producers were:

A. Take a moment to understand the joke, based on the
context, Nimesh's body language, tone, intent, and nuance.

or

B. Let themselves get triggered by some words and throw
a group temper tantrum.

They chose B, and in turn missed a big opportunity to laugh
and to allow the queer black men in the audience to be validated.

This is a perfect example of "It's All About You" Syndrome, which is sweeping our nation. I think the saddest part is that it's coming from the left. The right doesn't give two shits if you're insulted by their beliefs or rhetoric, but the left acts like an exposed nerve. They've become the PC police, and they should know better—they're supposed to be the smarter party.

Fran Lebowitz once said, "Being offended is a natural consequence of leaving the house." Homosexuality is definitely not a choice, but being offended? That is 100 percent a choice! Aren't jokes supposed to make you think? If you are always worried about someone hurting your feelings, then you're probably walking around armed and ready to be offended. What a fucking waste of time! People who go through their day constantly feeling hurt or outraged often react by trying to silence the people who make them feel that way. You want to know who really makes you feel bad? YOU! Get the fuck over yourself. The world doesn't revolve around you.

Years ago, I did this joke:

Did you guys hear about those Hasidic rabbis in Borough Park, Brooklyn, who were convicted of laundering Columbian drug money through their synagogue and yeshiva? I think they are innocent, because those Hasidim don't launder anything.

This prompted a woman to write me a letter about how the Nazis called us "dirty Jews" and that's exactly what I was doing as well. I was promoting anti-Semitic propaganda.

One day, I'm sitting on the subway, and a woman sitting across from me asks, "Are you Judy Gold the comedian?" I said yes, waiting for the usual "you're hilarious" comment. But no, it was her. Yes, HER—the writer of the letter equating me with Nazis. (God, why are you doing this to me?)

Why did I tell that joke? To make people laugh! Hasidic men do tend to wear long woolen coats and hats—even in the summer. I've seen my share of them looking a bit sloppy, with stains on their ties and crumbs stuck in their beards. Can we just say that a lot of the time, they don't present as camera-ready, they're not polite, and they seem to wear the same thing every single day? Besides, not one of them will ever hear that joke, so give me a fucking break.

I get so angry about this because I travel all over the country and never shy away from talking about being Jewish. I've performed in places where there are few to no Jews. Sometimes I'm the only Jew the audience has ever seen in person. I'm making them laugh, and perhaps opening their eyes and minds to thinking, *Hey, maybe those people aren't so bad after all*. That's the power of comedy.

Here's another joke I used to do that would set off the trigger alarms of the PC police:

> I travel a lot. And when there's a Jew in the audience, I can
> always tell. Because it's a thing we have . . . a feeling we
> get. It's an ethnic thing. I'm telling you Jews can always tell
> if someone is Jewish just by looking at them. We're just like
> black people. Black people can pick other black people
> out of crowds, and Jewish people can do the same thing.

The usual reaction to this joke was lots of laughter with a few select audience members looking at the black people in the audience to see if they were laughing, which would give them permission to laugh, too. Lighten up, people!

The funny thing about that joke is that it's true. There are many light-skinned black people who regularly pass for white, but my black friends can always tell. If you don't believe me, just ask Roseanne Barr.

3

You Suck!
Get Off the Stage!

I am, as I've said, merely competent.
But in an age of incompetence,
that makes me extraordinary.

—BILLY JOEL

hate people who are shitty at what they do for a living. I don't care what your job is—if you're getting paid to do something, make an effort and take pride in your work. Apathy and carelessness are so unattractive.

Take this scenario: On a friend's recommendation, you make reservations at a hot new restaurant. You arrive anticipating a delicious dinner. The waiter shows up a full ten minutes after you've been seated, but you let it slide, allowing that he's probably a little behind since the restaurant is new, and he's doing the best he can. You ask him what he thinks of the sea bass special, to which he responds, "I'm not into fish," and you can't help noticing that he rolls his eyes when your wife asks if the burrata appetizer is big enough to share. When he takes forever to bring your drinks, blaming the delay on the bartender, you find yourself losing patience, but thank him politely, trying not to let his lackadaisical attitude ruin your experience. A full fifteen minutes after he takes your order, he returns to the table to tell you that the entrée you selected is no longer available. You can barely contain your aggravation, but you don't want him to spit or pee in your food. Then he takes forever to bring out your appetizers, citing a "problem in the kitchen" (which you know he made up because you saw him scrolling through his Instagram feed until the manager yelled at him to stop). Either unfazed or unconcerned, he doesn't make any attempt to try harder, making it clear he thinks he's meant for far greater things than serving you dinner.

In truth, the food, drinks, and ambiance were actually excellent and the rest of the staff was working hard to make the place a success. But because of the horrendous service you received—the fault of one incompetent asshole with zero work ethic—everyone associated with the restaurant suffers the consequences of you, the customer, leaving dissatisfied. Plus, you weren't able to enjoy any of it.

Understandably, you have absolutely no interest in returning to that restaurant. Even though the meal itself was actually awesome, that one crappy employee ruined everything for you. There's a current of anger and resentment in the opinion of the place that you share with your friends (who then share your impressions with others). You may even share your experience on social media or post a critique on Yelp, encouraging who knows how many potential patrons to forgo giving the restaurant a try. The only bright side is fantasizing about pouring a bottle of red wine over the waiter's head while he chokes on the cold bacon-wrapped date stuffed with gorgonzola that you left on your plate.

No matter the field, incompetent practitioners hurt their profession's image. The same is true in comedy. Bad comics do, indeed, make it harder for the rest of us—especially when we have to follow them onstage. Substituting shock for humor, bullying people, denigrating women and minorities, inciting hatred, and, worst of all, writing shitty and lame material gives other stand-ups a bad name. Have you ever witnessed a seasoned comic with killer material struggling onstage? Oftentimes it's because a lousy comic earlier in the lineup created a bad tone and pissed off the crowd. When this happens, audiences become more guarded, are reluctant to participate, and are inhibited about laughing. This makes our job much more difficult. There's a phrase we use—"getting the audience back"—that refers to those times when we have to pick up the piles of shit that the previous comic left on-stage before we can go on with our set. Like anyone else, comics can have a bad day—or night—at work. I try never to blame the audience, but the same factors that can fuck up your day, ruin your commute, or take the pleasure out of an activity can affect a stand-up comic's set. Just think about all the vitriol continuously spewed out in our country right now. Haven't you noticed that more people are on edge, acting rude, and lashing out? If you don't think that comes from our orange headliner in chief, you're wrong.

The one great thing about being a Jewish comedian is that Jews love to laugh. There are tons of Jewish organizations, community centers, synagogues, philanthropies, and groups that hire comedians for their big galas or fund-raisers. It's part of our culture. I tend to perform for a lot of charities because I believe in the Jewish philosophy of *tikkun olam*—healing the world. I think laughter is a big healer, and if I can raise money for a great cause by making people laugh, I'm all for it. This isn't as easy as it sounds. I cannot tell you how many times I've had to perform after a depressing speech or video at a fund-raiser. Sometimes it's like, "Six million Jews were slaughtered in the Holocaust . . . *And here's your comedian, Judy Gold!*" It's a good thing I've been doing this long enough that I can make a joke about it to disarm the audience.

In the mid-1990s, I was booked to headline at a club in Marietta, Georgia. After the feature act ended his set, the MC came back onstage and did two jokes. The first was about Lorena Bobbitt, who'd cut off her abusive husband's dick. The gist of the joke was how the police officers searching for John Bobbitt's penis wouldn't want to pick it up off the ground (because a guy touching another guy's cock is so disgusting). The punch line went, "You pick it up." "No, *you* pick it up." "*I'm* not picking it up!" Kill. Me. Now. The second joke was about how the MC and his brother used to measure their feces in the toilet to see who'd delivered the bigger one. "Hey bro, come and look. You can't beat that!"

After these two highbrow bits, he introduced me, and I took the stage. At the time I had really short hair, and I'd open with a joke about how everyone always thinks I'm a transvestite (that word was in use at the time):

> At the gym, I walked into the ladies' locker room. This naked woman sees me and hides behind her locker. Then she says to me, "Oh, I'm sorry. I thought you were a man." So, I whipped it out! I showed her my penis.

The audience groaned. After a few nights of this happening, I lost it. "Wait a minute!" I said. "So this guy can talk about John Bobbitt's dick, and the size of his and his brother's shits, and I can't say 'penis'? What the fuck is that about?" A woman in the audience came up to me afterward and thanked me.

I can't tell you how awful it is being on the road, away from family, friends, and all of the comforts of home, and after your first show, you realize that the folks in your audience aren't *your* audience. This happens often before you've developed a following and people don't know what to expect. And it also happens when a booker hires the wrong people to open for you. I've had bookers purposely hire hacky male comics to open for me just to make it harder for me to get laughs. Misogyny? Perhaps, but that's hard to prove. There's nothing worse for a comic than staying alone at a crappy hotel and rising each morning in anticipation of having a tough time onstage that night. You have the entire day to obsess over your show, so you tend to spend lots of time calling your comedian friends for emotional support. (Before cell phones, laptops, and other low-cost means of connecting with people long-distance, time crawled, and it was torture. Just sitting here writing about it gives me a stomachache.) Feeling stranded and unappreciated keeps a lot of comics off the road, and even makes some quit stand-up altogether. For many of us, the only way to make a living doing stand-up is to schlep out of town to beer-soaked and grease-stained clubs that pay a decent salary for the week. If the gig sucks, you have to try to forget about it and hope the audience at the next job will love you.

Doing a set on a late-night television show in front of a studio audience that's been put in the wrong mind-set for your material is an entirely different story. TV doesn't afford the comedian the luxury of leaving knowing that only a few comics and 150 random people witnessed their bad set. Nope. It's out there for all the world to see—in perpetuity.

I was booked on *The Tonight Show with Jay Leno* on March 2, 2000—a time when a successful appearance on a late-night show could lead to lots and lots of bookings. I was nervous, even though I'd overprepared. Of course, I was also excited. Jay came by my dressing room before the show to say hello. He's a really nice guy. The name on the dressing room next to mine was "Senator John McCain." At that time, the senator was also a Republican presidential candidate, fighting George W. Bush for the GOP nomination. Naturally, McCain had been in the news a lot, but that particular day's edition of the *New York Times* featured an article about him apologizing for referring to Pat Robertson and Jerry

Falwell as "forces of evil." McCain said it was meant as a joke, but of course that comment was the only thing anyone wanted to discuss with him.

It's nerve-racking when you're finally booked on a show you've dreamed about being on for your entire life, only to end up following a serious talk about politics. The senator's segment consisted of a discussion about the Christian wrong—I mean, right— the politics of division, and his apology to Robertson and Falwell. Hilarious! *This next guest is a really tall, funny lesbian who will be talking about her overbearing Jewish mother. Ladies and gentlemen, please welcome, comedian Judy Gold!!!*

I got some decent laughs, and after my set Jay invited me over to the sofa to chat, but I remember feeling like the studio audience just wasn't in the mood for me. I'd achieved one of my goals, but it wasn't on my terms. I'm pretty certain that if I'd followed an interview with Isaac Mizrahi or Madonna, it would've been a different experience entirely. I share this story to illustrate how factors out of a comedian's control can affect the way they're received. Booking McCain was a great get for *The Tonight Show,* and I'm sure helped their ratings, but it certainly didn't help me. You go to a club or theater looking forward to being entertained by live stand-up comedy—the booking of offensive, unfunny, and unprepared comics ruins it for everyone. Of course, in our country, everyone has the right to say whatever they want onstage, but when we give a platform to mediocrity, nobody wins. So please, don't make the good guys take responsibility for the unfunny assholes.

4

I Didn't Say
They're *All* Cheap

Embrace what makes up you.
Some stereotypes are true—I love
chicken, but that's a stereotype, I
love fucking basketball, but that's
a stereotype, too. But who cares?
Embrace it. Be who you are, and don't
be ashamed of what that is.

—ICE CUBE

'm often asked during interviews, "Are you more of a lesbian comedian or a Jewish comedian?" I want to respond, "What the fuck kind of stupid fucking question is that?" but I don't because I want a good write-up.

The truth is, I'm a Jew who happens to be a comic, and I'm a comic who happens to be a lesbian—whom I love is part of who I am—but being a Jew is all of me. It's the way I look, what I eat, how I talk, what I feel, and how I think. It's in my DNA—literally. I grew up in a Jewish household full of stereotypes, including the overbearing, guilt-inducing mother, the quiet CPA/attorney father, arguments, sarcasm, and lots of food. I never saw my parents drink liquor unless we were invited to a wedding or bat or bar mitzvah or during the Jewish holidays, when we downed Manischewitz Concord grape. In terms of alcohol consumption, at least, many of my Irish friends had an entirely different experience growing up. Is that a coincidence? Doubtful.

Human beings are complex, and nobody can be reduced to a label, but stereotypes don't just assemble out of thin air. Recognizing that fact acknowledges that we're all, to varying degrees, products of our ancestry. Our predecessors are our legacy, and hopefully one day in the future—if this world still exists—we'll be a part of someone's legacy, too.

"Did you say that you currently live in Scarsdale? Ohhhhh, that explains a lot."

It's understandable that someone might take offense to being categorized, but that stereotype paints a picture that is, indeed, worth a thousand words. When you hear someone described as a "goombah," chances are your brain conjures up an image approximating Tony Soprano. The phrase "Latin bombshell" likely brings to mind a woman more or less like Sofia Vergara; a thousand-word summary detailing this bombshell's appearance, speech, movement, attitude, etc., isn't necessary. Of course, there are some stereotypes that are sick, destructive distortions of the past, and when they're perpetuated by hacky, ignorant, lazy comics, it's not only insulting, it discredits our profession.

The Jews

Let's take my people first. We'll start in the Middle Ages, because if we go all the way back to "Let there be light!" or the big bang, there will be no end to this book, and I have shit to do. You might recall that at the time, the Christians were not huge fans of the Jews. They thought we were odd people who prayed incorrectly. They also accused us of poisoning wells, spreading the plague, and using the blood of Christian children to bake matzoh. And they somehow got it into their heads that we killed Jesus. (That this is still used as a reason to hate us is maddening. Nobody alive today was there, so we don't know the full story! Can we please move on already? Do I blame every single German person born before 1930 for the Holocaust? Well, maybe a little.)

During the Middle Ages, Jews were deliberately isolated from the mainstream and denied the same rights as Christians. Jews weren't allowed to own land and were excluded from most professions. One business Jews were allowed to engage in was money-lending. Though charging interest on loans made it possible for Jews to make a living, when they came to collect what was owed, they were not welcomed—probably in the same way my American Express bill isn't welcomed. And so, they gained a reputation for being cheap. Now, continuing to disparage us for five hundred years because some of our people were just doing their jobs seems ridiculous, when you think about it. But is this why there were—and are—a good number of Jews employed in banking? And why some, like the Warburgs and the Rothschilds, were able to amass prodigious wealth? Probably. I'm sure their ancestors handed down their shrewd negotiating tactics and financial smarts (two things completely outside my purview, bolstering my point that no stereotype is completely accurate), so the reputation of Jews being obsessed with money is somewhat earned (pun intended). Jack Benny had a great bit about that:

CRIMINAL: Your money or your life.
BENNY: [*pause*]
CRIMINAL: Look, bud. I said your money or your life.
BENNY: I'm thinking it over.

Throughout history, Jews have been discriminated against, persecuted, scapegoated, ghettoized, expelled from their homes, and, oh yeah, packed into cattle cars, sent to concentration camps, separated from their children, tattooed with indelible numbers, used for medical experimentation, and sent to die in gas chambers. Centuries of living in such a state of uncertainty would have a profound effect on anyone, an effect they'd pass on to their children and their children's children. What could be more terrifying than knowing your kids are in mortal danger? Ergo, the overprotecting, overfeeding, constantly worrying, and doing everything possible to make certain that their children will be financially secure and accepted, even respected, by non-Jews. It's no wonder that traditionally Jewish mothers have been relentless when it comes to making sure their sons receive the best education possible and their daughters marry the most successful husbands (except if they're lesbians—God forbid, *pooh, pooh, pooh*). Oh, and Jewish fathers? They don't get many opportunities to speak.

Given the hardships and horrors we've endured, of course we have resorted to humor to bolster ourselves against the constant hostility surrounding us.

> In the Jewish faith, when does a fetus become a human being? When it graduates medical school.
>
> ▬
>
> JEWISH KID: Ma! Ma! I got cast in the school play!
> MOTHER: Oh, how wonderful! I'm so proud of you. What role did you get?
> KID: I'm playing the Jewish father!
> MOTHER: Now, you march right back there and tell them you want a speaking part!

Classic Jewish jokes like these and thousands of others have been around for ages, and have been told over mah-jongg and bridge games, at bar mitzvahs, seders, weddings, shivas, graduations, and anywhere else Jews gather together, from Miami Beach to the Lower East Side.

Jews brought up by stereotypical Jewish mothers are inclined to be anxious, neurotic, and guilt-ridden—consider *The Mary Tyler Moore Show*'s Rhoda Morgenstern, *Murphy Brown*'s Miles Silverberg, *Seinfeld*'s George Costanza, and *Friends*'s Ross Geller.

These fictional characters were the first introduction to Jews for many people in America. How is Jewish guilt different than Catholic guilt? It comes from your mother, not your religious beliefs or your rabbi. My theory is that Jewish guilt is survivor's guilt, since so many of us have perished just for being born Jews. Children of Holocaust survivors in particular suffer from debilitating guilt, as do children of Ruth Gold. We tend to never fully relax or trust that the good times will last. Woody Allen's neurotic persona didn't just pop out of his head. As his character Alvy Singer explains to Annie Hall in the rom-com by the same name, "I feel that life is divided into the horrible and the miserable." I can certainly relate to that.

Even at Jewish weddings, joyous occasions for most, one or both of the spouses break a glass at the end of the ceremony to remind us of the destruction of the temple in Israel. "Look, we all know you're young, in love, and about to start your life together, but don't forget that the first temple in Jerusalem was burned to the ground by vicious Babylonians who murdered, raped, and enslaved our people. Have a great life!! Let's eat, drink, and dance!!"

The good thing about all this is that like most marginalized people, Jews tend to have well-developed senses of humor. As my very enlightened mother put it, "If we weren't laughing, we'd be crying."

There are a number of other stereotypically Jewish attributes that can't be denied. Many of us do have big noses, astigmatism, curly hair, and nasal voices. The majority of us tend to see the glass as half empty or completely empty, or don't see the glass at all due to our poor eyesight. (Admittedly, there are also some optimistic Jews who see the glass as *only* half empty.) We tend to be vocal about what we want and need—especially in restaurants. A lot of us are doctors, lawyers, teachers, and bankers, and some are even Jewish American Princesses (JAPs), and many of the jokes about us were originated by and circulated among ourselves. "What do Jewish women make for dinner? Reservations." We appreciate the importance of music, art, and theater, but don't let your son become a performer unless you want him to starve. We love sports even though we're not the best at them, and since there's more than a 1 percent chance you're going to get hurt playing a sport, Jewish mothers are wary of them. Many agents and managers in show biz are Jewish due to our excellent negotiating skills, which were honed over a thousand years ago. I say all this with authority because I see the world through Jewish eyes. When a comedian has a deep understanding, knowledge, perception, and awareness about something—especially themselves—they tend to find the real funny. No one does this better than Richard Lewis:

> My grandmother was a Jewish juggler: she used to worry about six things at once.
>
> I've always been a hypochondriac. As a little boy, I'd eat my M&M's one by one with a glass of water.
>
> I tried phone sex and got an ear infection.

There's a bit I used to do in my act about a message my mother once left me on my answering machine after we got disconnected and I neglected to call her back. I was at my agent's office, where I would often make long-distance phone calls because they were free. (Yes, children, we had to pay more for a call to New Jersey from New York City, and we also had to go home and check the answering machine to retrieve any phone messages that were left for us while we were out.) I was living in my current apartment building/shtetl, where everyone knows everyone's personal business. My next-door neighbors, Sy and Marjorie Cohen, remain my neighbors to this day and are the godparents to my children. So, after my mother and I got cut off, I ran some errands, then took the subway home. When I played my answering machine, here's what I heard:

MOM: [*hysterical*] Judith! Are you all right? Did you fall down? What happened? Where are you? I'm a wreck! I don't understand this. Maybe I'll call Marjorie and tell her to go over and find out what happened. JUDITH!! WHERE ARE YOU?!?!?!? [*pause*]
[*sotto voce*] So long.

What is that "so long" at the end of the message? She thinks Jeffrey Dahmer has chopped my body into a million pieces, and she says, "So long"? This, my friends, is an example of imprinted behavior—the result of trauma passed down through generations of Jewish mothers. My poor mother was particularly distressed. Her tendency to default to expecting the worst possible scenario was reinforced by the memory of the sudden and tragic death of her fourteen-year-old brother. That's not funny at all, but her reaction was, and that's what comics focus on—the funny.

African Americans

Brought to America as slaves in the seventeenth century, African Americans were kept illiterate, being taught only enough to be able to perform their forced labor efficiently. Once freed, their educational opportunities were severely limited by racist laws that affected their employment and economic opportunities. Jim Crow kept them apart from whites socially. Naturally, those conditions led to the emergence of new dialects, ones that, of course, included phrases, pronunciations, and usages that sounded "uneducated" to the privileged white majority. This gave some credence to the black ghetto stereotype. And unfortunately, since poorer neighborhoods tend to have more crime as a result of higher unemployment and inadequate safety nets, the stereotype of African Americans being involved in criminal activity germinated. When you're sent to a country that considers you three-fifths of a person, you're faced with hurdles others can only imagine. Being stripped of your dignity and then being freed into a mostly unwelcoming society, you do what you need to do to get by. And if you think the systemic racism in this country isn't also passed down from one generation to the next, you're sadly mistaken. That's a big reason why there are so many great black comedians. Tragedy plus time equals comedy.

WANDA SYKES

I'm not politically correct. I still say "black," I do. Because "African American"—there's no bonus; it's not going to make your life any easier. You don't see black people standing around going, "Woo yeah, African American. Man, I tell you, this beats the hell out of being black. We should have made the switch years ago."

DAVE CHAPPELLE

Every black American is bilingual. All of them. We speak street vernacular and we speak job interview.

CHRIS ROCK

Every town has the same two malls: the one white people
go to and the one white people used to go to.

RICHARD PRYOR

I went to Zimbabwe. I know how white people feel in
America now—relaxed! 'Cause when I heard the police car,
I knew they weren't coming after me!

DICK GREGORY

A guy comes up to me, says, "I'm from Mobile. I sure
enjoyed your act. You ought to bring it to Mobile." I need
to take my act to Mobile like Custer needed more Indians.
Like the Rev. Martin Luther King needs a convention of
dime-store managers. I won't even work the southern part
of this room.

One of the first African American comedians happened to be
a woman. Moms Mabley, born Loretta Mary Aiken in North Carolina in 1894, was one of sixteen children. By the time she was fifteen years old, both of her parents had died in tragic accidents and
she'd been raped at least twice, resulting in two children she gave
up for adoption before running away to join a minstrel troupe.
She performed in the Chitlin' Circuit, a collection of performance
venues for African Americans during the vaudeville era, until she
was accepted and eventually came to be beloved by white audiences. She was a social critic and civil rights icon, as was Dick
Gregory, and their humor enlightened many. They owned their
stereotypes, just as they owned those privileged white audiences
who paid lots of money to see them perform.

MOMS MABLEY

I was on my way down to Miami . . . I mean They-ami. I was ridin' along in my Cadillac, you know, goin' through one of them little towns in South Carolina. Pass through a red light. One of them big cops come runnin' over to me, say, "Hey woman, don't you know you went through a red light?" I say, "Yeah I know I went through a red light." "Well, what did you do that for?" I said, "'Cause I seen all you white folks goin' on the green light . . . I thought the red light was for us!"

Women

Where to begin? Subjugated by men and limited politically, economically, and socially for thousands of years, we still don't make as much money as men. Apparently having a prostate and limited communication skills makes you more valuable as a human being. Due to our inferior status, women have had to find inventive ways to take care of themselves and get their needs met. So, it's not surprising that the idea that women were devious and not to be trusted would develop.

Historically, men have objectified women—and still do—yet accuse women of using sex, one of the few tools available to women in the past, to manipulate them. To this day, plenty of straight men have no idea how to have a platonic relationship with a woman, let alone have a conversation with one. Don't forget, women couldn't vote until 1920, couldn't get credit cards until 1974, could be excluded from juries until 1975, and could be fired for becoming pregnant up until 1978. Most women accepted these restrictions and found satisfaction—or at least faked satisfaction—in being a wife, mother, and homemaker. Snooze.

Onstage, male comics got away with degrading women, and female comics tended to be self-deprecating in order to disarm the audience before they gave it right back to the men. I know you're glad times have changed. All I can say is #MeToo.

Along with Moms Mabley, Jean Carroll, born Celine Zeigman in 1911, was one of the first women to write and perform traditional stand-up comedy. After winning an amateur contest at the age of eleven, Carroll entered the vaudeville circuit as a singer and dancer. By the time she was twelve, she'd kicked her abusive alcoholic father out of the house and was supporting her entire family. She graduated high school at fourteen and soon after joined the act of comedian Marty May. In the early 1930s, she went on to do a two-person act with her soon-to-be husband, Buddy Howe. The couple continued to perform together until he was drafted in 1943. After that, it was just her, an audience, a stage, and a microphone. This was a first. In the June 16, 1991, issue of the South Florida *Sun Sentinel,* Jane Wollman wrote an article about Carroll explaining that

> Because she was the only woman working that way, everyone said she "worked like a man." Indeed, to the press she was "the female Milton Berle," "a distaff Joey Faye," "a female Bob Hope, Charlie Chaplin, and Sam Levenson." . . .
>
> Carroll was accused of "competing" with male comics.
>
> "I didn't think of it in terms of competing," she says. "It never occurred to me that only men were supposed to talk."
>
> Courageous? She says courage had nothing to do with it.
>
> "I didn't say, 'My God, I have to go out there and do battle against the male species.' I knew I was funny, and I just did it."

As the first woman doing male-type stand-up, Carroll was also unfairly accused of copying male comics.

Of course, she was, but as it turned out, a very young Alan King actually stole one of her jokes.

Being attractive was a "handicap," Carroll says. "Once I heard a woman at ringside say, 'Oh, I don't think her legs are so great.' After that I realized good looks were a distraction, so I started wearing long gowns and covering up my body as much as I could.

"In those days, the attitude was, 'Let's see how funny you are!' because I was a woman and wasn't ugly and didn't make an ass of myself up there. The trick was to get the audience—especially the women—to feel I wasn't a threat," and to get past men's resistance that women weren't and shouldn't be funny.

"So, I did a little self-effacing material," she says. "You mix your herbs and spices, and pretty soon people are relaxed, and you've disarmed them."

Jean Carroll was way ahead of her time and was a big influence for many female comedians—especially Lily Tomlin. She ended up retiring because, she said, she loved her family more than show business. She talked about her husband and her rotten child while misogynist jokes like these were the standard fare in men's clubs and boardrooms across America:

How do you know when a woman is about to say something smart? When she starts her sentence with, "A man once told me . . ."

—

How many men does it take to open a beer? None. It should be opened by the time she brings it.

Now that women comedians have followed in Carroll's footsteps, it's more like:

ELAYNE BOOSLER

I'm just a person trapped inside a woman's body.

TINA FEY

Gravity is the story of how George Clooney would rather float away into space and die than spend one more minute with a woman his own age.

JOAN RIVERS

I blame my mother for my poor sex life. All she told me was, "The man goes on top and the woman underneath." For three years my husband and I slept in bunk beds.

CHELSEA HANDLER

Men don't realize that if we're sleeping with them on the first date, we're probably not interested in seeing them again either.

One of my favorite Jean Carroll jokes is:

The thing that attracted me to my husband was his pride. I'll never forget the first time I saw him, standing up on a hill, his hair blowing in the breeze—and he too proud to run and get it.

Carroll had the guts to say things that most women, at that time, could only think about their husbands. As women became more empowered, more female comics entered the fray. Women were becoming more educated and self-sufficient, and were realizing career and personal goals. No longer was June Cleaver the prototype for the American woman. Gloria Steinem said it best: "A woman without a man is like a fish without a bicycle."

Get over it, guys. We all do just fine without you.

Other Common Stereotypes

JAPANESE PEOPLE ALWAYS HAVE CAMERAS

For years, Japan's been at the forefront of electronic manufacturing, and the largest producers of cameras—Nikon, Panasonic, Fujifilm, Sony, Olympus—are all Japanese companies. Plus, many of the Japanese citizens we see here in the US are on vacation, which is when people are most likely to take photographs. Duh. So, the development of the stereotype is not surprising.

AFRICAN AMERICANS ARE THE BEST ATHLETES

The idea that African Americans are more gifted athletically than other groups stems from the same kind of thinking that concludes that all Chinese people are really good at math, all Italians talk with their hands, all Irish are lucky, and all gay men love Broadway musicals. While it's true that African Americans are well represented in most major sports leagues, the stereotype's reinforced socially when African American children are encouraged by parents and others to view a career in professional sports as one of a limited number of ways out of poor socioeconomic circumstances (which, we know, is an inequity rooted in our country's long history of racism and discrimination).

ASIAN MEN ARE MORE FEMININE THAN OTHER MEN

Of course, this is absolute bullshit. The image of Asian males as effeminate began to take root in the 1850s when the first Cantonese workers—a group comprised mostly of men—arrived in the United States. Americans of European descent saw the slight builds and hairless faces of the new immigrants as feminine, a perception that was reinforced by the newcomers' cultural practice of sporting long braids—compulsory in China—and wearing long silk gowns. With the nation's economy stimulated by the discovery of gold in California, and the shortage of women in the West, these Chinese immigrants found a niche working as cooks, launderers, and domestics—jobs considered "women's work." Despite later proving themselves adept at traditionally masculine labor, such as mining and construction, the stock figure of the emasculated Asian male has endured. Unfortunately, sometimes, old stereotypes die hard.

GAY MEN ARE PROMISCUOUS

I know many gay men. Some are promiscuous, and some aren't. But let's be real. We know that most men think about sex constantly. When there are two men in the relationship, that pretty much doubles the time. Since, until recently, gay men have been excluded from the institution of marriage (and its traditional expectation of monogamy), they've been free to hook up with one another without a lot of drama. Of course, a lot of them are having much more sex than the average straight person. Jealous?

AS I SAID EARLIER IN THIS CHAPTER, we're all products of our history, and stereotypes—earned or not—are part of our legacy. We can laugh at them for the spark of truth they contain, and we can, and should, challenge them when they've been unfairly assigned or used to denigrate. Of course, one of the best ways to challenge long-held yet false beliefs is with comedy.

For decades, comedians stereotyped gay men as sissies and used jokes to ridicule them. Similarly, lesbians were reduced to the butch stereotype. For the most part, their actual sexuality wasn't discussed (at least not in any way we'd think of as positive). The first comedian to come out onstage was Robin Tyler. It was the 1970s, and she was one half of the lesbian feminist comedy duo Harrison and Tyler. Robin ventured out on her own, and ended up not only performing stand-up but producing events for LGB rights (calm down; there was no *T* or *Q* yet!), women's rights, and the anti-war and AIDS movements. She was an activist not only through her actions but also through her comedy. One of my favorite lines of hers is, "If homosexuality is a disease, let's all call in queer to work: 'Hello. Can't work today, still queer.'" Robin was way ahead of her time and never got the recognition she deserved, which is an unfortunate indicator of how society dealt with—or rather, didn't deal with—homosexuality.

In 1981, Kate Clinton started doing stand-up, performing material about politics, growing up Catholic, and being a lesbian. A few years later, some other LGB comedians, tired of not being able to talk honestly about who they were, took the big step of coming out onstage. These comedians brought their true selves to the audience, and though they definitely made some audience members uncomfortable, they enlightened and put many more at ease. One of them was my best friend, Bob Smith, or as my kids called him, Uncle Bob. He was tall and handsome, and resembled a young

Jimmy Stewart. He came out onstage in the mid-1980s, joking, "I made my carefully worded announcement at Thanksgiving. I asked my mother, 'Could you please pass the gravy to a homosexual?' She passed it to my father. A terrible scene followed."

Soon other LGBT (there it is folks! Q coming soon!) comedians were talking about their sexual orientation in clubs and on TV. In 1988, Bob teamed up with fellow stand-ups Jaffe Cohen and Danny McWilliams to form the group Funny Gay Males. They performed all over the world, including the Just for Laughs comedy festival in Montreal. In the early 1990s, Frank Maya appeared on MTV's *Half Hour Comedy Hour* and Lea DeLaria appeared on *The Arsenio Hall Show*. In 1994, Suzanne Westenhoefer and Bob became the first openly gay and lesbian comedians to get their own HBO comedy specials. Bob went on to become the first out comedian to perform on NBC's *The Tonight Show*. Their jokes were smart, funny, and biting:

BOB SMITH

> I was raised Roman Catholic, and according to the Catholic Church it's okay to be homosexual as long as you don't practice homosexuality. Which is interesting, because I think it's okay to be Catholic as long as you don't practice Catholicism.

SUZANNE WESTENHOEFER

> This guy stands up and says, "Hey, did you get that way because you had some kind of bad sexual experience with a man?" I'm like, yeah. If that's all it took, the entire female population would be gay.

I recently corresponded with a British comedian who, at the age of thirty, found out that she was an intersex person. She was married at the time and wanted to have kids but had never gotten her period and was having trouble getting pregnant. It turned out that her ovaries weren't ovaries at all. They were made up of testicular tissue. So, she changed her name to Amazon and came out onstage as intersex. When she told some fellow comedians in the UK that she was going to be coming out onstage, they weren't very support-ive. One commented that she'd make the audience uncomfortable. In reality, it was *him* she'd be making uncomfortable. HE'S uncom-fortable? How fucking selfish! What about how uncomfortable she felt hiding her true self? Using humor to explain who she really is—now *that's* what stand-up's all about.

I asked Amazon how long it took her to gain the confidence to talk about it onstage (and yes, she uses "her" as a pronoun, so calm the fuck down): "I found out at age thirty and came out at age forty. It did take ten years of processing the news of my identity and overcoming the hermaphrodite stigma. I thought there was no place that existed in society for someone like me. I actually decided to come out following a sexism dispute I witnessed."

And here comes the power of comedy—the power to disarm and erase the stigma. Amazon humanizes something that makes other people feel ill at ease by making them laugh: "What I will tell you is that I have a genetic form of intersex, and that means that externally I've got the body of a woman, but I've got the genes and brain of a man. That means I'm crap at housework and I like to spend a lot of time playing with my titties."

This joke only scratches the surface of who Amazon is. Her use of a common denominator—no matter how simple—opens the door to discussion on a subject that people feel uncomfortable (yet super curious) about. Secrecy causes shame. Plus, her body is a gift, comedy-wise—not as a target for laughter, but as a platform to share with others the unique way she experiences the world.

Amazon told me that lately she's been focusing more on activism than comedy: "Even though they've taken my gonads, I need the balls to fight social injustice." You can be sure that her comedic chops will only help her to reach more people and hopefully break the stigma once and for all.

It wasn't until 1973 that homosexuality was removed from the list of mental illnesses by the American Psychiatric Association—1973!! I turned eleven that year. I already felt different than other kids. I had no interest in girly things. I wanted to mow the lawn, shovel the snow, go to Rickel Home Center with my father. I hated home economics class, where we were required to learn how to cook, sew, clip coupons, and perform other wifely duties. I wanted to take shop class, learn how to drive, and play kick the can with the guys. Even before it was scientifically proven, I knew deep down inside that I was born this way. I also knew from social cues that I could never, ever tell anyone.

The years I spent in the closet were horrible. I felt like a fraud. I couldn't eat. (Hmmm, maybe I should go back in for a few months.) I loved my out gay male friends. They were fearless, fun, and, yes, fabulous. Then the AIDS crisis hit. I was a sophomore at Rutgers University in New Jersey when the first cases were reported. Junior year, I came out to my closest college friends—and they came out back! How weird that the people I chose to hang out with all turned out to be gay, gay, gay!!! We spent the summer out, proud, and stoned while listening to the original Broadway cast recording of *Pippin* on a loop. (I know. I'm a big queer sucker for show tunes.) I finally felt like I could be the real me, but by the middle of my senior year, I started fearing for my gay male friends' lives.

I moved to New York City after college. It was 1984, and I lived in a brownstone on West Eighty-First Street with a gay opera singer who traveled a lot. I used "The Gay Roommate Service" to find him and the apartment because I wanted to feel safe being myself at home. It turned out that for the LGBT community, there was a lot that wasn't safe—especially sex.

My posse and I took care of sick friends and watched them, along with acquaintances and coworkers, die. We witnessed some parents reject their child's surviving partner, forbidding them from attending their beloved's funeral. Some of the deceased's families claimed their children's property, leaving their grieving partners homeless. As the AIDS movement made financial and medical strides, many people on their deathbeds suddenly took a turn for the better. A lot of them recovered fully after new drugs were introduced. But there were—and still are—hundreds of thousands not so lucky.

Carol Henry was a close friend of mine, as well as a hilarious comic. She'd contracted AIDS from shooting heroin with a dirty needle. She refused prescribed medications, taking a holistic approach instead. She'd go to these crazy doctors who'd give her unconventional, off-the-wall cures. She went on a juice diet, drank her own urine, and did a lot of other weird and desperate things.

Carol spent the last months of her life at her mother's house in Rockland County, New York. I'll never forget visiting her there. On one visit, she looked at me with her emaciated face and said, "I feel so old." Her mother, Anne, immediately chimed in, "Well, of course you do, you're forty-one years old!" I thought Carol was going to drop dead right there. She'd been knocking ten years off her age for as long as I'd known her. This was the '90s, before Google made it impossible to lie about your age, your education, your job, or your secret second family. Though she was weak, Carol was so pissed off that she screamed at her mother. I said to her, "Carol, I can know you have full-blown AIDS from shooting up in some guy's bathtub, but you can't tell me your real age? WHAT THE FUCK?" We laughed. Because that's what you're supposed to do.

Comedian Steve Moore brought his HIV/AIDS diagnosis to the stage in the mid-1980s, at the height of the epidemic. By inviting audiences to laugh with him, Steve allowed them to put aside their fears of the virus. He encouraged them to see that each AIDS case was, in fact, a person—in Steve's case, a warm, smart, and wonderfully funny person. Watching someone joke about having such a cruel and ruthless disease helped audiences put their own lives into perspective:

> People always say, "My God, you look great. I can't believe you've been exposed to the AIDS virus. You know, you've never looked better!" Oh really? Well, pretty soon I'll be drop-dead gorgeous . . . I love it when it gets quiet. I'll just mess with people even more.
>
> ——
>
> Don't fuck with me. I'll open a vein and take out the whole front row.
>
> ——
>
> I come home for Christmas two years ago and my mom, Wilma, buys me a cemetery plot. I'm not kidding. Isn't that sweet? Thing is, I come home for Christmas last year and my mom doesn't give me anything. And I said, "Hey Wilma, what's up with that?"
>
> "Well, hell, you didn't use what we gave you last year."

Comedians use stereotypes ironically, sarcastically, self-deprecatingly. As with all fraught language, it's the comic's responsibility to generalize appropriately—otherwise, it's all about hate. But stereotypes aren't going to disappear because we pretend that they don't exist. Good comics will dispel stereotypes in surprising and clever ways. When they do, it's okay to laugh at those parts of yourself that fit a stereotype and to join with others in laughing at those parts of themselves. Jeff Foxworthy has made a career—and a shitload of money—out of embracing the cartoonish stock image of the uneducated, unsophisticated, redneck Southerner. By doing so, he's gotten audiences to acknowledge and laugh at the seed of truth in the stereotype while at the same time showing the absurdity of painting every American below the Mason–Dixon Line with the same brush.

> If your favorite topless bar is the one where your daughters work, you might be a redneck.
>
> ——
>
> If you put ninth grade on hold while you started a family, you might be a redneck.
>
> ——
>
> If your fourteen-year-old smokes in front of her kids, you might be a redneck.
>
> ——
>
> If *The Jerry Springer Show* asks you back, you might be a redneck.

If you're at a comedy club and a comedian is using negative stereotypes that reinforce your opinions, then you can be sure of two things: the comedian sucks, and you're a racist, misogynist, anti-Semite, homophobe.

It also goes to say that if a stereotype doesn't apply to all Jews, African Americans, women, Asians, gays, lesbians, Southerners, etc., it follows that it doesn't necessarily apply to you. Look, I'm a six-foot-two Jew. How many people think, *Oh, she's Jewish? She must be really tall*. I'm gonna go with zero.

Finally, when a comedian makes a joke about a specific person who happens to display a stereotypical behavior, the joke is about that particular person—not the entire group. If you're offended by proxy because you happen to work with a Jewish mother who's not overbearing, that's your choice. Look, our natural impulse is to protect ourselves and our children from harm and unpleasantness, but the world is full of amazing, beautiful, and hilarious things that sometimes make us uncomfortable.

Laughter is a release, and it's good for you. Barricading ourselves in "safe spaces," where even the slightest possibility of discomfort is intolerable, leaves us emotionally stunted and, dare I say, unhappy. And FYI, if my mother isn't offended, why are you?

5

Sometimes the Truth Hurts

There are only two mistakes one can make along the road to truth: not going all the way, and not starting.

—BUDDHA

C omics are pretty low-maintenance—unless you're our parent, spouse, child, or work in customer service. But seriously, performance-wise, we're easy. All we need is a microphone, an audience, and hopefully a stage to do our thing. Flip on the lights at a comedy club, and chances are it's filthy and the mic smells disgusting. Stand-up's a dirty profession on many levels. It's not sweet and sultry like cabaret, beautiful to watch like ballet, or respected like theater. It doesn't carry you away like music. It catches you off guard and jars you. It's basic. Simple and powerful.

Since I've done a bit of theater, I'm often asked what the difference is between acting in a play or musical and performing stand-up. To me, the difference is glaringly obvious: an actor has to keep the audience's attention, but a comedian has to *get* the audience's attention. Think about it. At a theater, you're given a program as you're guided to your seat. You get comfortable and turn off your cell phone. Then the house lights dim and the curtain goes up. A while later, after the actors have taken their bows, you exit in an orderly fashion. At a comedy club, you're shown to your table, where you order your required two beverages and possibly some pub food. During the performance, everybody's drinking and eating. Servers are running around, people are getting up to pee, there's chitchat. Occasionally there's a heckler or two. Then, near the end of the show, checks are thrown on the tables (the dreaded check spot—when no one pays attention to the comic onstage because they're all doing math in their heads or on their phones to check the charges or calculate the tip). As soon as the headliner's set ends, the club starts blasting music so the audience will leave quickly and can be replaced by a newer two-drink-minimum audience. It's not pretty.

Stand-up can be especially ugly with an unappreciative audience or, worse, a comic who's phoning it in. Seasoned pros are constantly editing themselves during their performances. If I'm headlining a room and open with a political joke, and the audience isn't into it, I'll veer away from politics. Actually, I did the following joke at a gig in Florida:

> Trump is so awful. He's the only human being in the entire world who could make American Jews want to move back to Germany. *[pause, then, as if I'm talking to the Germans]* "Hi, guys. We're back! Yeah, it was going great and we don't know what happened, but we heard you guys are sorry, so here we are! Listen, I left some artwork here I was hoping to get back. Silverware? Grandparents?"

The early show booed and hissed at this bit, and then made me work my ass off to get a laugh. The late crowd, on the other hand, loved the joke, and I ended up having an amazing set. Yes, I could've made a conscious decision before I went onstage to refrain from telling that joke to a bunch of older Jewish Floridians, but I love that joke. It's funny and relevant. Of course, no one in the audience took the extra second to fully understand the joke—they were triggered because I mentioned Jews and Germany together—and, oh, they were Trump supporters. I ended up having to adjust my material, pleasing the audience enough so I'd be able to return to my hotel without any visible injuries. Performing for people who've decided that they personally dislike you is utter hell when you're doing stand-up, because it's such an intimate art form. When you go to an art gallery, do you love each and every painting by the artist? If not, do you walk around the gallery with a puss on your face, uninterested in seeing any more of the artist's work? When you go to hear music, do you love every single song the band plays or the singer sings? Do you completely check out for the rest of the show once you've heard a song you don't particularly like? I highly doubt it.

A friend of mine recently told me about a concert she attended about ten years ago. In her early fifties, she went back to college to get her master's degree. Outside one of her classrooms, she saw a flyer advertising that Jackson Browne was coming to do a concert on campus. He had recently put out a new album, and since she was a huge fan, she immediately purchased tickets. This would be at least her sixteenth time seeing him live.

At the concert, he started off playing songs from his new album. Then he continued playing songs from his new album. People were disappointed and started yelling, "Do the old stuff!" "'Pretender'!" "'Running on Empty'!!" "'Stay'!!" But to the chagrin of his old fans, he kept on performing his new material. My friend stayed for the entire concert and doesn't recall people leaving en masse, but she wasn't happy. We all understand this; the familiar is comforting. But art isn't all about comfort—especially for artists. Why? Because, as they gain more life experience, their art reflects their growth, mirroring who they've become. Some fans were undoubtedly dissatisfied with the show, but I'll bet that Jackson Browne was completely satisfied performing new music he'd undoubtedly been working on for a significant amount of time. Quite an accomplishment for a sixty-year-old guy who could be living very comfortably off of his past earnings.

Comics are not musicians with hit songs, so most people want to hear new material when they go see a comedian they're familiar with. True comedy fans may enjoy hearing the same bits over and over again, but most people want to hear a joke once (and then repeat it to their friends, incorrectly and with bad timing, so they get no response and have to say something like, "Well, I don't know the exact words he used. Anyway, you had to be there."). There are some comedians who see stand-up purely as a job. They work on the road or as the house MC/comedian for a casino, or they perform on cruise ships fifty weeks a year, doing the same act every night. That's a perfectly fine way to make a living, but there are those of us who'd seriously die inside if we couldn't do stand-up. In 2015, I was a panelist on the short-lived *Nightly Show with Larry Wilmore*. The topic was vaccinating your kids. I'm a huge proponent of vaccinating—in fact, my mother's great-uncle, Dr. Joseph Goldberger, cured pellagra. Some of his research was used to find treatments for malaria and led to the development of other vaccines. (Pardon me as I try to impress you with my proximity to greatness.) That parents would put their children—and other people's children—at risk of contracting a potentially deadly disease because of bullshit "science" promoted by some B-list celebrity is dangerous, selfish, and plain stupid. After the panel argued the merits of getting vaccinated, Larry posed a loaded question to each of us. Panelists had to answer the question as honestly as possible. If Larry and the audience believed you were being 100 percent honest, you would get a "Keep It 100" card to take home. If Larry and the audience felt you were dishonest, you would get a weak tea bag. The question Larry posed to me was, "You can vaccinate your kids, but you can never do stand-up again. Or you can do stand-up, but only if you don't vaccinate your kids." My answer? "Sorry, kids!" I won the "Keep It 100" prize.

For so many great comedians, stand-up is in their blood. It's their life's work. You rarely hear about comedians retiring. Look at George Burns, Joan Rivers, Milton Berle, Don Rickles—the list goes on and on. What keeps most comedians working into their eighties and nineties? The fact that we have something new to say. Any seasoned stand-up knows how to work a room and please the masses, but oftentimes, when we do that at the expense of what we actually want to talk about, we feel like we're selling our souls. Imagine Picasso being required to create paintings for the rooms in a Marriott, or Diane Arbus needing to use her talents to take high school yearbook photos, or Irving Berlin having to write a jingle for a United Airlines commercial. DO NOT GET ME STARTED ON THAT ONE! What a waste.

In the days before social media, comics became famous in vaude-ville or on the radio before television changed the game. Everyone watched TV and often a great set on Ed Sullivan, Steve Allen, or, later, Johnny Carson made someone a star. As we know, they had to be clean and abide by the FCC regulations, which could be stifling for someone who had much more to joke about than a wife who's a horrible cook or a husband who's too lazy to take out the garbage.

When certain comedians became disheartened with pleasing audiences just to get the job done, they made the crucial decision to speak openly about their lives and the critical issues affecting them, us, and the world. They used language deemed verboten, and though they ventured into territory that made audiences un-easy, these brave groundbreakers broadened the conversation and ultimately made us begin to better understand one another. They wholly believed in the First Amendment and used it to tell the truth.

When you mention the concept of freedom of speech to any comedian, usually the first name that comes out of their mouth is Lenny Bruce. Lenny is the Jesus Christ of the First Amendment as it relates to comedy—he died for our sins, or at least took a lot of the punches, stabs, and bullets. Lenny was born Leonard Alfred Schneider in 1925 and grew up on Long Island. That's almost a hundred years ago, and yet his act would be considered controversial in today's PC climate.

On the totem pole of entertainers, comics are near the bottom, along with strippers, lounge singers, and Times Square Elmos. Actually, plenty of comedians started in strip clubs, where they'd introduce the strippers and tell jokes between their acts. (Honey Bruce, Lenny's wife and the mother of his daughter, Kitty, was a stripper.) When you're a new comic, it doesn't matter where you perform, it's *that* you perform—anyplace, anytime. Getting up onstage is the only way to learn the craft.

Lenny started out innocently enough as a comic doing impressions, one-liners, and other safe material. But as his act developed, not only did his style change, he also began to discuss the issues that were most important to him.

His voice pattern was different than that of most comics of the time. He didn't have that predictable cadence so common among his contemporaries. He was a great storyteller, and his love of jazz was apparent in the way he performed his bits. Sometimes he'd go off on a riff, improvising, then shake his head, surprised at where he'd gone.

ON SEXUALITY:

If you believe there is a God, a God that made your body, and yet you think that you can do anything with that body that's dirty, then the fault lies with the manufacturer.

ON HYPOCRISY:

I've been accused of bad taste, and I'll go down to my grave accused of it and always by the same people, the ones who eat in restaurants that reserve the right to refuse service to anyone.

ON MISOGYNY:

That's where the conflict starts. We all want for a wife a combination Sunday school teacher and a $500-a-night hooker.

ON RACISM:

You are a white. The Imperial Wizard. Now, if you don't think this is logic, you can burn me on the fiery cross. This is the logic: You have the choice of spending fifteen years married to a woman, a black woman or a white woman. Fifteen years kissing and hugging and sleeping real close on hot nights. With a black, black woman or a white, white woman. The white woman is Kate Smith. And the black woman is Lena Horne. So, you're not concerned with black or white anymore, are you? You are concerned with how cute or how pretty. Then let's really get basic and persecute ugly people!

ON POLITICS:

Liberals can understand everything but people who don't understand them.

ON RELIGION:

Every day people are straying away from the church and going back to God.

One might say that Lenny pushed the envelope by tackling topics most other comics wouldn't touch. In reality, he used words people avoided outside the safety of their own homes to prod them into dealing with issues they'd normally steer clear of. (His first arrest, in San Francisco, was for using the word *cocksucker* onstage.) He made people uncomfortable because he exposed all their bullshit. He held up a mirror to the social issues that most white Americans wanted swept under the rug, and he did it in a satirical way. What could be more effective than someone using truth and humor to call you out on your hypocrisy? There's no way you can defend your point of view without so obviously becoming the butt of the joke.

In the court documents that Lenny would read onstage after his arrests, he was accused of being obscene, indecent, immoral, and impure. By the end of his life, he was banned from several US cities. How crazy is that? This is the United States of America, where people come from all over the world to be free to practice their religion, voice their opinions without consequences, pursue the lives they want, and live with dignity. Sorry to tell you folks, but it's been over two hundred years, and that's still not the case here.

Lenny on all the legal *mishegoss:*

In the Halls of Justice, the only justice is in the halls.

In March 1964, Lenny made his third appearance on *The Steve Allen Show*. At the time, Steve Allen was a fierce defender of the First Amendment, although in his later years he was very vocal about conflicts between his anti-censorship beliefs and vulgarity and immorality on television. On this particular episode of his show, Allen gives Lenny a four minute introduction, warning viewers about what they're going to see tonight. Allen insists that Bruce is not a comedian who tells dirty jokes. Instead, "he deals with subject matter which many people consider off limits. Religion. Sex from the philosophical viewpoint. Things that will shock you." He goes on to suggest that if his viewers don't want to be shocked, they should turn the show off for the next ten minutes. "Go watch Johnny Carson. Or the late night movie. (Although ten minutes of it won't do you much good.) Go out in the backyard and have a beer, if that's what you do. Go in and kiss the kids if they're asleep. Go do something constructive. But don't sit there and then send me a stupid postcard."[1]

Lenny begins his act by saying, "I have a reputation for being sort of controversial, and irreverent, and also the semantic bear trap of bad taste . . ." He goes on to tell the audience not to worry, because he is going to behave. And he did. He didn't curse, though he would later be arrested for using profanities in clubs. But those weren't the words Lenny found offensive. The words that offended him were "words like Governor Faubus [the racist Arkansas governor who called in the state's National Guard to prevent the integration of public schools], segregation, nighttime TV, well, not ALL nighttime TV—shows that exploit homosexuality, narcotics, and prostitution."

The real threat wasn't Lenny's use of profanities in public, but the substance of his repertoire. He was telling the truth, the often-uncomfortable, sometimes-horrible truth. He made people think. That being said, every single comedian who gets up onstage and curses owes Lenny Bruce a shitload of fucking gratitude.

Lenny was good friends with Mort Sahl, another political satirist. Unlike Lenny, Sahl was nonthreatening. He didn't curse, and he often brought a newspaper onstage to use as fodder. Steve Allen described him as a political philosopher. Sahl contended, "Comedians have to challenge power. Comedians should be dangerous and devastating—and funny. That's the hardest part."

Sahl dressed academically and was featured regularly on network television, as opposed to Lenny, who made only six TV appearances during his entire career. Yet as different as they were, *Time* magazine labeled them both, along with fellow comics Shelley Berman, Mike Nichols, and Elaine May, "sickniks" and their humor as "sick."[2] Just because of their penchant for underscoring behaviors that made people unconformable. Sick comics! Let that sink in. These guys are telling the truth and making people laugh, and they're basically being called morally corrupt. You know what's morally corrupt? Censorship.

A few more of Sahl's brilliant lines:

I'm for capital punishment. You've got to execute people. How else are they going to learn?

—

Liberals feel unworthy of their possessions. Conservatives feel they deserve everything they've stolen.

—

There are Russian spies here now. And if we're lucky, they'll steal some of our secrets and they'll be two years behind.

—

Those who learn nothing from history are condemned to rewrite it.

Sahl was the prototype of many political comics we see today, but Lenny Bruce's influence on stand-up and censorship is beyond measure. Would there have been a George Carlin or a Richard Pryor without Lenny? Who knows?

Carlin's story and Pryor's have a lot of similarities. Both started out as clean, suit-and-tie-wearing, conventional stand-up comics. Pryor had modeled himself after Bill Cosby. (I should really say that he modeled his *comedy* after Cosby's, not his behavior. I think we can safely say that Pryor's leisure activities did not include drugging and raping women.)

Tangent Time!

I'm sorry, but I have to vent. You're Bill Cosby—you're a fucking national treasure! Do you really need to sedate women to get them to sleep with you??? And how fun can that be? Don't you want some feedback while you're having sex? Did he think the women would wake up and be like, "Oh my! I must have fallen asleep. Excuse me, Mr. Cosby. Now, what were we saying? Oh dear! My shirt seems to be unbuttoned. I'm such a mess today."

Bill Cosby is a horrible person, but he was a great comic. Whenever he's mentioned, I'm reminded of Denis Leary's joke, "Ted Kennedy, a good senator, but a bad date." You cannot deny that Cosby is a comedy genius, but offstage, he was a predator, a rapist, a liar, and a hypocrite. He should be the brand ambassador for cognitive dissonance. I will never hear his comedy the same way ever again.

Okay, I'm done. Thanks for indulging me.

At any rate, Carlin's and Pryor's first TV appearances were on *The Ed Sullivan Show* and *The Merv Griffin Show,* respectively. They both did various impressions and other non-edgy and nonthreatening bits. Carlin grew up in New York City and was raised by his mother, a devout Catholic who'd left his well-to-do alcoholic father. He dropped out of high school at fifteen. Pryor was brought up in Peoria, Illinois, in a brothel run by his grandmother. His mother was a prostitute and his father was a pimp. His childhood was one of poverty and abuse. At fourteen, he was expelled from high school. Carlin joined the air force. Pryor joined the army. I tell you this because these experiences informed their views of the world.

Their TV appearances put them in top-notch clubs, and they each might have had careers like Cosby had they stuck to comedy that was noncontroversial. But how could they have done that, considering where they came from? They each had a drastic metamorphosis onstage in Las Vegas.

For Carlin, it happened at the Frontier Hotel, where he had a two-year contract making $10,000 a week. It was 1969, and $10,000 a week was a lot of money. (For 99 percent of us, it still is.) This particular night, he was doing an early show for an audience he referred to as "some golf assholes." His set included a bit about how he had no ass—and because he used the word *ass,* he was canceled. It seemed as if he was canceled to please the rich golf assholes, who were spending a lot of money at the Frontier. The hotel said they'd pay Carlin the full value of his contract, even though there was an entire year left on it.

The following year, they decided to bring Carlin back for another engagement. That time, he said the word *shit* onstage: "You know, some people say shit. Buddy Hackett says shit, Redd Foxx says shit, I don't say shit. I smoke a little of it, but I don't say it." For that, he was fired. FIRED! In 1970, when there were race riots and Vietnam War riots going on, a comedian used the word *shit* and it was the end of the world.

Pryor's first major epiphany occurred at the Aladdin hotel on the Vegas strip, where a battle that had been brewing between his true persona and his stage persona came to a head. The story goes that Pryor was onstage and in the middle of his act when he looked out into the audience and saw the Rat Pack sitting there (some say it was specifically Dean Martin—whom my mother had a huge crush on). From the way they were looking at him, Pryor realized that to them, he was just a joke. Pryor then walked off the stage, but walked off in the wrong direction. The stage manager told him to go the other way, but he said, "No, I'm not walking out on that stage again." Perhaps what he really meant was that the Richard Pryor to whom the stage manager was speaking would never again be walking out onto any stage from that moment forward.

Both Carlin and Pryor suffered because of their steadfast commitment to authenticity. As Pryor said:

> In those days, I was basically lying to myself about what I was doing. I kept asking myself, "How can I do this, how can I do this?" I saw how I was going to end up. I was false. I was turning into plastic. It was scary . . . so I did what I had to do—get out of that situation. I was blackballed by most of the industry for two or three years after that.

There are still topics and words that are taboo on network TV, so thank God for cable. We all owe HBO a lot for putting uncensored comedy on TV in the 1970s. After their respective Vegas experiences, when Carlin and Pryor were onstage, they were free. Pryor needed to talk about race and poverty. He'd learned to use language as a coping mechanism during his difficult childhood. In his act, he used language as a weapon. His imitation of white people was so funny because he exposed their denial of their prejudices.

Carlin didn't want to be a fool. He'd gotten a big appreciation for the English language from his mother. His famous bit, "Seven

Words You Can Never Say on Television," is classic: shit, piss, fuck, cunt, cocksucker, motherfucker, tits. (I can't believe you still can't say "piss" or "tits" on network TV.) Read them aloud: shit, piss, fuck, cunt, cocksucker, motherfucker, tits. They're just words—words that for some reason cause fear and anxiety in people. WORDS! Carlin said, "There are 400,000 words in the English language, but only seven of them that you can't say on television. What a ratio that is! 399,993 to 7. They must be really bad."

Carlin was arrested in Milwaukee in 1972 because an off-duty police officer heard him doing his bit onstage at the Summerfest music festival and was appalled by it. The officer was with his nine-year-old son and couldn't understand why no one was doing anything about Carlin's obscene behavior. He called his commanding officer and got permission to arrest Carlin after his show. This wasn't the first time Carlin had been taken to the precinct. In fact, during one of his arrests, he shared the back seat of a police car with Lenny Bruce. Carlin had been in the club when the police were arresting Lenny. When an officer asked Carlin for his ID, he said that he didn't believe in government-issued IDs. And there he went.

Like Carlin, Pryor was a prolific writer. He wrote for *The Flip Wilson Show* and *Sanford and Son,* and won an Emmy for his writing work on CBS's comedy variety show *Lily,* starring Lily Tomlin. Both men were irreverent, and like Lenny Bruce, they paved the way for every comedian to say what they want to say onstage. Carlin professed, "I think it's the duty of the comedian to find out where the line is drawn and cross it deliberately." In 1975, *Saturday Night Live*'s creator and producer, Lorne Michaels, wanted Pryor to host an episode of *Saturday Night Live*, then in its inaugural season, but by that time Pryor had developed a reputation for unpredictable behavior, having previously ad-libbed obscenities, shown up on set completely wasted, and even assaulted an NBC page. Since

SNL was a live show, the network executives were scared that he'd say or do something forbidden on network television that would be broadcast to millions of living rooms. When Michaels declared that he could not produce a contemporary comedy show without Richard Pryor, the network came up with the idea of a five-second delay. This would give them time to censor whatever came out of the comedian's mouth. Today, the delay is still used for live television, although it's actually seven seconds.

I especially loved it when Carlin talked about religion. "The only good thing that came from religion is the music." That's funny. And when you think about how religion has affected the world since the beginning of recorded time, you might agree—especially if one faith or another was shoved down your throat when you were a child. What Pryor and Carlin witnessed in their lives exposed them to blatant hypocrisies that fed their psyches and made them incredible social commentators.

There are a substantial number of comics who don't want to make waves because they just want to make a living, and as I said before, that's just fine. I am not one of those comics. It doesn't feel right for me to compromise my beliefs because I might offend someone. I've been doing stand-up my entire adult life, and I have something to say. I'm offended every day by ignorance, stupidity, and incompetence. So when I see young people—especially those college bookers who dictate what comics can and cannot say onstage (trigger warning)—I want to smack them and say, "You've lived in this world for twenty years. Take a step back, shut up, live a little, and fuck your feelings."

6

Lighten the Fuck Up!

It is a curious fact that people are
never so trivial as when they
take themselves seriously.

—OSCAR WILDE

Humor is just another defense
against the universe.

—MEL BROOKS

I spend Memorial Day through Labor Day in Provincetown, Massachusetts, where my days consist of playing tennis, swimming, working out, writing, and performing stand-up a few nights a week at a small theater. During the summer, I love catching up with everyone at the tennis club—especially those who come back to play for just a week or two each year. At a round-robin tournament, a guy reminded me of the last time we played together. "Do you remember? It was a couple of years ago." I told him that, in fact, I did remember him. It was the day of the Carnival Parade—Provincetown's version of Mardi Gras, but much smaller. He continued, "The theme for Carnival that year was the eighties, and you told me that you were dressing up as a distressed T-cell." (That certainly sounded like something I'd say.) "Whenever I tell that to people our age, you know, the ones who lived through the AIDS crisis, they think it's hysterical. But when I tell young people, they're appalled." I responded, "Yeah, because we know the pain so deeply, it's practically the only way to cope. That's one of the main points of my book!!!"

COMEDY CAN BE USED as a shield to deflect anger, judgment, and hate. I can't think of anything worse than a world without laughter. BORING! Jokes and satire are tools that encourage us to see a situation from a new perspective, and when they're wielded by someone with a profound understanding of that situation, the jokes are even funnier and more healing.

Numerous times in my life, I've brought up a sensitive subject with someone, only to have them shut down. "I'm just not ready to talk about that yet." Of course, when this happens, I feel like shit for overstepping a boundary, but the truth is that it's not about me at all. It's about their level of comfort and trust. When a comic broaches a touchy topic onstage, the audience needs to trust her—and she needs to be comfortable and knowledgeable about that particular issue. And the joke better be fucking side-splitting.

In our pluralistic society, pretty much everyone's an outsider, whether because of their race, religion, national origin, gender, gender identity, sexual orientation, size, political leanings, mental or physical capabilities, age, trauma, family history, or some combination thereof. Comedy is a powerful device that can inform, persuade, incite, motivate, rally, teach, and bring people together. Believe it or not, comedians are responsible for educating millions about important ideas. Their material influences people's opinions—opinions that'll be shared and, hopefully, inspire action.

For sixteen years, *The Daily Show with Jon Stewart* was a major source of news—and opinions—for millions of (mostly younger) viewers who tuned in each night. Twice, Stewart was included in *Time* magazine's list of the hundred most influential people in the world. Comedians Samantha Bee, Bill Maher, John Oliver, Stephen Colbert, Seth Meyers, Stewart's *Daily Show* replacement Trevor Noah, and others continue enlightening viewers about newsworthy events. Jimmy Kimmel's late-night monologues attacking the

Graham–Cassidy healthcare bill were instrumental in the bill's ultimate collapse. Satire and humor are incredibly effective weapons when it comes to fighting or defending against dangerous and destructive realities.

Here are a few brilliant examples (well, more than a few, because they are, indeed, brilliant) of how these comedians used humor to raise awareness on serious, complex issues:

JON STEWART

Religion. It's given people hope in a world torn apart by religion.

—

You have to remember one thing about the will of the people: it wasn't that long ago that we were swept away by the Macarena.

—

Divorce isn't caused because 50% of marriages end in gayness.

—

The [Supreme Court] ruling that anyone who's arrested—even accidentally—can be strip-searched was decided five to four, with the votes for the searches coming from the Court's five conservatives. You know—the "defending personal liberty" guys. Which is weird because I'm not a constitutional scholar, but I'm willing to bet big government feels its biggest when it's inside your anus.

JOHN OLIVER

Drug companies are a bit like high school boyfriends. They're much more concerned with getting inside you than being effective once they're in there.

Campaign ads are the backbone of American democracy, if American democracy suffered a gigantic spinal injury.

Sex is like boxing: if one of the parties didn't agree to participate, the other one is committing a crime.

SAMANTHA BEE

Christmas: it's the only religious holiday that's also a federal holiday. That way, Christians can go to their services, and everyone else can sit at home and reflect on the true meaning of the separation of church and state.

After a generation spent successfully riling up the base with feverish anti-abortion rhetoric, it's no surprise that the divisive issue has divided many from their own sanity. Since 1977, self-appointed soldiers of God have visited abortion providers, with 185 incidents of arson, 42 bombings, 100 acid attacks, 26 attempted murders, and 11 actual murders. You know, pro-life stuff.

On Mitch McConnell blocking Obama's Supreme Court nominee's appointment: Let's just have a Supreme Court vacancy for a year because some chinless dildo wants a justice who will use his gavel to plug up your abortion hole . . . Filling court vacancies is one of three jobs a president actually has: appointing justices, bombing the shit out of the Middle East, and turkey pardoning. That's it.

———

Discussing representatives blocking a proposal for the ability to use Supplemental Nutrition Assistance Program (SNAP) benefits for diapers: Oh my God, conservatives, make up your mind about poor babies. We thought you wanted them to be born. Why else would you oppose free contraception, wage jihad against Planned Parenthood, fight the FDA on Plan B, and make abortion as unattainable for poor women as a ticket to *Hamilton*? Well, like it or not, there are a lot of poor babies, and it seems all you got for them is the same useless advice you're giving their mothers: Keep your legs crossed. Hypocrisy exhibit A.

STEPHEN COLBERT

If our Founding Fathers wanted us to care about the rest of the world, they wouldn't have declared their independence from it.

———

Contraception leads to more babies being born out of wedlock, the exact same way that fire extinguishers cause fires.

———

I believe that the government that governs best is a government that governs least, and by these standards we have set up a fabulous government in Iraq.

BILL MAHER

In this country, you're guilty until proven wealthy.

———

If you have a few hundred followers and you let some of them molest children, they call you a cult leader. If you have a billion, they call you "Pope."

———

The tea-baggers. The one thing they hate is when you call them racist. The other thing they hate is black people.

TREVOR NOAH

Donald Trump didn't invent racism. Trump didn't invent Islamophobia. And he didn't invent violence. All he did was put his name on it like he does everything else.

———

Juggling is such a white thing, when you think about it. No, just the whole concept—you have so much stuff that, at some point, you're like, "I can't even hold all of this stuff! I'll have to throw some of it in the air!" That's probably how juggling started. Someone was like, "Wow, you have three things, but you only have two hands. Would you like to share something with me?" "No, no, I'll figure it out."

ELLEN DEGENERES

If more gay people would endorse, well, not in a commercial, but although . . . could you imagine? "Hi, I'm Ellen DeGeneres and I'd like to talk to you about Gay. Do you find yourself in love with, attracted to, or just curious about the same sex? Maybe it's time you try Gay. You'll notice a difference in as little as forty-eight hours. I should know. I'm not just the spokesperson, I'm a Gay. Side effects may include loss of family, loss of friends, and unemployment."

PAULA POUNDSTONE

Gay Republicans, how exactly does that work? "We disapprove of our own lifestyle. We beat ourselves up in parking lots."

EVERY DAY WHEN COMEDIAN GERI JEWELL, who has cerebral palsy, was in college, she took a bus to class. One day, when she was upset about flunking math for the third time, Gerry bumped into her friend Alex Valdez on the bus. She told Alex that she didn't want to be in school, that she wanted to be in show biz. She wanted to be like Carol Burnett. He said to her, "Why don't you do what I do? I go to The Comedy Store every week and tell blind jokes." (Just to be clear, Alex tells blind jokes because he's visually impaired and not because he's a colossal asshole.)

Geri was worried that the audience would only want her to talk about her cerebral palsy, but Alex advised her to read the newspaper, write material about current events, and then talk about what was on people's minds. He also told her to acknowledge her cerebral palsy when she first got up onstage, but then use the other material to "bring everyone into your world." That's what she did. She drove to the club, and Danny Mora, who was running the shows, put her onstage at about eleven P.M. He wanted to be certain that Mitzi Shore, legendary owner of The Comedy Store, was out of the room when Geri did her first-ever stand-up set. Danny wanted Geri to be solid and comfortable enough on-stage before Mitzi saw her perform.

The MC introduced Geri, saying something like, "Are you ready for the next act? He drove all the way from Orange County to be here tonight, so please welcome Geri Jewell!" He thought her name was "Jerry," so assumed she was a man. Geri didn't correct him. Instead, she got onstage and said:

> I don't know about you people, but I've been hearing
> a lot about all of these gay people coming out of the
> closet. [*silence*] But what you haven't heard about are
> all the cerebral palsy people coming out of the closet.
> [*silence*] Please don't tell anyone, it's our secret. Obviously,
> I know I have it, but you definitely can't tell Anita Bryant
> because she'll get on another bandwagon. All our children
> will be walking around like this.

The audience let out a big laugh, and when Geri finished her act, she got a standing ovation. Soon after, Geri got cast on the hit sitcom *The Facts of Life,* where she played Geri Tyler—Blair's cousin with cerebral palsy.

Just like Geri, Josh Blue and Maysoon Zayid both have cerebral palsy. Josh was the first comedian to perform stand-up on *The Ellen DeGeneres Show.* Maysoon is a Palestinian American Muslim comic and is the first-ever comedian to perform stand-up in Palestine and Jordan. Her 2013 TED Talk has been viewed by more than 15 million people. Brad Williams was born with achondroplasia, a form of dwarfism. He is a powerful presence onstage and has had two critically acclaimed Showtime comedy specials. Comedy fosters understanding. It can override objections and allow the audience to trust the comedian to take them outside their comfort zone. What makes these comedians great is that, although their material may be about them, it's *for* the audience. Their acts have put able-bodied people at ease and taught them that, in reality, people with disabilities are not much different from anyone else. As Maysoon states in her TED Talk, "People with disabilities are the largest minority in the world and we are the most underrepresented in entertainment." Hopefully, these performers are changing that—one laugh at a time.

Gary Gulman is one of the best comics in the business. His writing's impeccable, and his jokes are very relatable—especially for those who suffer from depression, like me. With Gary's permission, I'm quoting this chunk of his act in its entirety, because it is so powerful that it not only helps people unaffected by depression to understand it better, but shows those with the condition that they're not alone.

> Why is it so hard to get out of bed? I'll tell you why.
> Because the thing that they don't tell you about life
> growing up is this: Life—it's every single day. Every single
> day, you have to wake up and live and go through all
> the maintenance and the upkeep. Argh—I can't wait
> to have a caregiver. The thing that gets me through,
> though, is doughnuts and ice cream. I love ice cream,
> but I have this thing where I don't want to eat the entire
> pint, so I say, "Just eat half the pint." But then, when I get
> halfway through, I have this compulsion where I need to
> leave a flat surface. Who am I leaving the flat surface
> for? The day crew? They'll come in and be outraged by
> all the crags and crannies? But I find myself eating it
> flat. I eat more, and then I'll come across a chocolate
> chunk and I'll have to excavate that. And then there's a

pothole. I gotta smooth that over. I'm doing all this ice cream masonry work. Then it starts to melt around the edges—and that's delicious, so I have to eat that. Before I know it, I've hit bottom. Literally and figuratively, I've hit bottom. And I just finish the ice cream and put the fork down. More often than not, I use a fork to eat ice cream. And if you eat ice cream with a fork, I know you so well. I know you so well. Because my policy is, "I'm not washing a spoon until I'm all out of forks." And people say, "Why don't you just wash a spoon?" HAH! Why don't I shower? Fork prints in ice cream—if I see fork prints in your ice cream, I know your world. Fork prints in ice cream are evidence of a life in chaos. Chaos! If I see fork prints in your ice cream, I don't need to see your kitchen—I know the dishes are piled so high, you can't refill the Brita. Not that I should refill the Brita—I haven't changed the filter in four years. I don't need to go into your bedroom—I know there's no top sheet on your bed. The top sheet is tacked up over the window as a curtain. I don't need to go into your bathroom—I know that the new roll of toilet paper is resting on the empty spool. It's the only household chore I can do while sitting on the toilet. And I'm like, "Pfff! Not today, not today." I don't have the strength to squeeze that spindle and lock it in.

There are so many things in the world to be pissed off about, and skilled comedians know how to turn those things into jokes. Lewis Black, one of my all-time favorite people, once said, "I'm a happy person but an angry citizen." I can definitely relate to that. I mean, I host a podcast called *Kill Me Now* where celebrities talk about the things that make them crazy mad.

For years, I was furious that I didn't have the right to get married. I'd been out onstage talking about my kids and my family just like all married comedians do, but I wasn't legally married. I remember one performance in Texas where I talked about my kids, and a military guy approached me afterward to say that he finally understood why we were fighting for marriage equality. That encounter drove me to write a bit about all the horrible people who had more rights than me simply because they are heterosexual: Erik and Lyle Menendez, who each got married in prison while serving time for shooting their parents to death. And Mary Kay Letourneau, a teacher who raped one of her thirteen-year-old students and gave birth to their first and second children in jail. After her release in 2005, they got married and stayed married until 2019. HOW? Oh, and Jerry Sandusky, the pedophile Penn State football coach. He's entitled to a tax credit when his wife dies, and I'm not?? NOT FAIR!!! If that bit changed one person's vote—and I'm sure it did—then my act did more than make audiences laugh.

Comedy is powerful in so many ways. It can reduce anxiety and alleviate pain. How else could people deal with the world? If there's anything so horrible you can't joke about it, pray you never find out what it is.

Humor can get you through a tragedy—and life. In January 2018, my friend Bob Smith succumbed to ALS. He wasn't only a brilliant stand-up but also a respected and award-winning author. As the ALS progressed, Bob's arms and hands, paralyzed by the disease, dangled uselessly from his shoulders. In order to type, he'd shrug and drop his right shoulder, allowing his longest finger to land on a letter on his iPad. He wrote his last two books that way, laboriously, one letter at a time on an iPad, because it was too hard for him to press the keys on a computer. Bob never gave up, and even though he could no longer speak, he could laugh.

I'd say, "Bob, why the hell couldn't you just get AIDS instead of this fucking disease?" and he'd crack up. He experienced some gut-wrenching tragedies in his short life, but his fierce sense of humor allowed him to live each and every day with laughter. He lived with ALS—which kills most patients within three to five years—for over twelve years, and I'm sure it was his ability to joke about it that kept him alive for so long. I want to leave you with an excerpt from his excellent book, *Treehab*. I think this pretty much says it all:

"Lou Gehrig's Disease? I don't even like baseball!" My best friend and fellow stand-up Eddie Sarfaty claims that was my initial reaction when he accompanied me to Columbia-Presbyterian in 2007 to receive my you're-gonna-die-agnosis. I don't remember saying it, but I'm convinced one of the reasons I'm still alive is that good comedians naturally respond to Pain and Death as if they're hecklers trying to ruin our shows.

Many of my oldest and closest friends in New York are accomplished and brilliant stand-up comedians, but we've made each other laugh harder offstage than with anything we've ever said in our acts. The morning after my sister, Carol, committed suicide, Judy Gold called to see how I was doing. When I broke down crying uncontrollably, Judy matter-of-factly inquired, "Bob, don't you think you're overreacting? It's been almost twenty-four hours."

I didn't stop crying, but I did laugh. I've known Judy for thirty years and our friendship has no boundaries. One time, Judy called about forty-seven times, badgering me not to be late picking her up at the airport. To get even, I stood among the limo drivers waiting at the gate holding up a sign that said "bitch." I ignored the stares and whispers about my sign until I finally heard Judy laughing while simultaneously telling me to go fuck myself. Judy accusing me of overreacting is the perfect example of my belief that comedy is not frivolous but one of the most vital and serious aspects of being alive. Her making me laugh the morning after my sister's death was like lighting a candle in a coffin.

7

There's a Reason It's Called an "Act"

It's nice to have an elephant in the room. There's nothing more helpful than something everybody's thinking about.

—SETH MEYERS

Years ago, I was at a Christmas party where I didn't know many of the guests—no big deal, I'm friendly and struck up some conversations. The following day, when I called to thank the host, he told me that one of the guests had complained that I wasn't really funny at the party. What the fuck?

Actually, it's not uncommon for comics to get unsolicited feedback like that from "civilians." They only know us by our acts and expect us to bring our stage personas into social settings. These people know little to nothing about show business or respecting boundaries. If you were to attend a party and, say, Neil Patrick Harris was there because he's a childhood friend of the host, would you refer to him as Doogie Howser or Barney Stinson? NO! Because he's not the characters he plays on TV. You also probably wouldn't tell him that you played Harold Hill in *The Music Man* in eighth grade, or that your grandmother met Paul Lynde when she was a contestant on the original *Hollywood Squares,* or that your niece is in the other room and would love to do a monologue from *'Night, Mother* for him and get his opinion. Would you go up to Halle Berry at a cocktail party and say, "You know, I love all of your movies, but boy, *Catwoman* was a bomb, huh?" Not a fucking chance—unless, perhaps, you're a psychopath like Donald Trump.

Stand-up is an intensely personal art form, so it's understand-able that a small number of civilians might find it difficult at first to differentiate between the person onstage who made them laugh and the person they're introduced to in a social situation. But if, after a few minutes of conversation, someone still can't make that distinction, there's something wrong; it shouldn't be that tough.

I acknowledge, however, that in certain cases, drawing the line between a comedian and his or her onstage character can be especially challenging. Andrew Dice Clay, born Andrew Silver-stein, is such a case. Clay's character, Dice, is a macho, homophobic misogynist who degrades women, says anything and everything offensive, and is beyond politically incorrect. His filthy nursery rhymes are his trademark:

> Hickory dickory dock, some chick was sucking my cock.
> The clock struck two, I dropped my goo, and dumped
> the bitch on the next block.
>
> ⸺
>
> Twinkle, twinkle little star, will she blow me in the car?
> I bought her dinner, she had fun. My balls are boiling, I'd
> like to cum.

These rhymes are juvenile, filthy, and shockingly honest, but a moron wouldn't have the brains to write them, and people—including me—laugh at them anyway. They're so fucking stupid, yet making Mother Goose's innocent couplets as X-rated and of-fensive as possible is, in itself, brilliant. Plus, the lines are being recited by a sexist, homophobic Elvis! That's not who Clay really is. It's an act. If the audience can't see that he's playing a charac-ter, then they're the joke.

Before introducing Cher at the 1989 MTV Video Music

Awards, Clay did three minutes of stand-up that included his nursery rhymes, jokes about banging a 600-pound woman, and the words *shit* and *tits*. Afterward, he was banned for life from appearing on MTV. That ban never deterred him from doing his thing, and in fact, it kept him in the papers for two years afterward. It was eventually lifted in 2011, and in an interview for CNN.com the following year, Clay said, "Comedy is like the last art form where you can get up there and just do whatever you want. You know, like they say, you are the producer, director, writer, star. And if they take that away, you know, that's what America is, that's what we were built on, freedom."[1]

We can all agree that Clay's humor appeals to the lowest common denominator and that perhaps his use of the word *fag* in his bits wasn't the best decision—especially during the height of the AIDS crisis—but Clay stands by his (and his character's) right to say things the way he wants them said, maintaining that while using the word *gay* would be politically correct, the word *fag* is funnier and truer to his onstage persona.

In a 1990 appearance on *Larry King Live,* King asked Clay if a part of him enjoyed the attention he was getting from negative publicity. Clay's response was prescient. "I think it's too much. I think they've made too much out of a comedian because that's all I am, you know, I'm an entertainer. If I was saying . . . I'm running for president and saying those kinds of things, that's a different ball game." Or is it?

Clay is back in theaters doing his act. He's unapologetic and even more politically incorrect than before. This pleases his fans—old and new. Although his character is still a total misogynist, his current opener is a very funny woman, Eleanor Kerrigan. Eleanor is fearless, edgy, and confident. It might seem like cognitive dissonance for Clay to have a strong woman warm up his audience, but that tells you something about who he is as a person. I'm certain a small portion of the audience doesn't get that the profanity-filled buffoon onstage is not the real Andrew Silverstein. I'm also certain that as a comic, Clay would rather they did. Halfway through *Indestructible,* his 2012 special for Showtime, Clay remarks, "I'm a comic. This is what I fucking do. If I did three-quarters of the stuff I'm talking about up here, I'd be doing twenty-five to life in a maximum-security prison." Some people just don't get it.

Interestingly, while too many people have trouble discerning the difference between comedians and their acts, it doesn't seem nearly as hard for them to separate other artists from their work. They can like, or even love, someone yet hate their paintings, poems, or music. The reverse is also true.

During Coco Chanel's lifetime, she was idolized by people all over the world who adorned themselves with the designer's hats, clothing, makeup, and fancy perfume because, as she's known for saying, "In order to be irreplaceable, one must always be different." Wait a second. Different? I'm sorry, Coco, did you mean different like being a Nazi? Different like going on anti-Semitic tirades? Different like working for German military intelligence during World War II? Today, many wealthy people, including practicing Jews, still buy her products, and the Chanel brand is valued at nine billion dollars.

It's irrefutable that Michael Jackson was a musical genius. It's also indisputable that the descriptions given by the men featured in the HBO documentary *Leaving Neverland* of Jackson's repeated patterns of pedophilic behavior are sickening, to say the least. Still, people love his music. I get nostalgic listening to the Jackson 5 (though I have to confess that an eerie feeling comes over me when any of the songs Jackson recorded during the period covered in the film come on the radio).

Sometimes there's an additional price paid by a comic after he or she "comes out" about something onstage, and that is when audience members feel they should also "come out" to the comedian about themselves. You cannot imagine some of the comments, stories, criticisms, and thoughtless analyses that are forced upon comedians after a show. And why do people think that's okay? Why? I'm not your friend. I'm an entertainer, and you've paid me to share intimate details of my life with you. But the show is over, and if you want to pay me to listen to intimate details of *your* life, that's fine. But I'll need to fill out a W-9 and you'll have to make the check out to my agent. He gets 10 percent. Often, someone insists I listen to a joke or story that "you should use in your act." It's annoying—but fine. They're fans, and they're trying to be helpful. But frequently, after a show, I'll be approached by an audience member, telling me, unsolicited, "I really didn't like that Jeffrey Epstein joke." Really? Too fucking bad! Then don't laugh and shut up. Do you go up to Lady Gaga after a concert and say, "You know, I'm not crazy about that 'Poker Face' song"? For me, the most egregious double standard is when someone gets offended by a joke and then lets it ruin their enjoyment of a comic's entire act.

When I told people that I was writing a book about freedom of speech from a comedian's perspective, the question most frequently asked was, "Are you going to talk about Louis C.K.?" Yes! I wouldn't be doing my job here if I didn't talk about comics who've had to deal with fallout, whether from personal views they've expressed publicly or for abhorrent behavior offstage.

If you've been asleep for the past few years, I'd like to catch you up on some things that have happened in the world of comedy. In November 2017, Louis C.K. admitted to sexual misconduct after the *New York Times* printed the stories of four women who claimed that Louie had masturbated in front of them, and another woman who said he did it while on a business call with her. Within hours of the story's release, the premiere of Louie's new movie *I Love You, Daddy* was abruptly canceled, as was an appearance on *The Late Show with Stephen Colbert,* where he was scheduled to promote the film.

Louie penned a response to the allegations, acknowledging their validity. Here's a portion of his confession, which was also published in the *New York Times:*

> These stories are true. At the time, I said to myself that what I did was O.K. because I never showed a woman my dick without asking first, which is also true. But what I learned later in life, too late, is that when you have power over another person, asking them to look at your dick isn't a question. It's a predicament for them. The power I had over these women is that they admired me. And I wielded that power irresponsibly. I have been remorseful of my actions.

Immediately after the piece was published, FX dropped its hit show *Louie* (where I once played a married lesbian whose pregnant surrogate went into early labor after fucking Louie), FX Productions canceled its overall deal with Louie's production company, and the network stripped him of his titles on the four shows he produced, as well as his cowriting gig (with his good friend at the time Pam Adlon) on the series *Better Things*. Louie was subsequently dropped by his manager, agent, and publicist, and all streaming comedy specials, films, and reruns involving Louie disappeared. Just weeks prior to the *New York Times* report about Louie, accusations of sexual abuse regarding Harvey Weinstein and Kevin Spacey had been reported and confirmed. Three weeks after the *Times* piece, TV hosts Charlie Rose, Matt Lauer, and Senator Al Franken all found themselves unemployed.

The #MeToo movement is no joke (pun intended). Not only were Louis and his staff affected financially, our close-knit comedy community was deeply affected emotionally. The situation forced a well-needed, candid dialogue and debate about something far too prevalent in comedy workplaces, which lack HR departments and where drug and alcohol use are common.

Comedian and writer Laurie Kilmartin wrote an op-ed that appeared in the November 10, 2017, edition of the *New York Times*—the same day Louis admitted his bad conduct. Kilmartin gives the reader a thorough and vivid description of what it's like to be a woman working in stand-up in the USA:

> Standup comedy is hard on its women. I started in 1987 in San Francisco. Since then, I've worked mostly with male comics, for male club owners. I've wiggled out of thousands of uncomfortable hugs and let my cheek catch a kiss meant for my lips. I don't have a story about misconduct by Louis C.K. like the ones that five women recently told reporters (which he admitted are true), and no one has masturbated in front of me, at least not without my consent. But I'd say almost every female comic could name a comedy club she can't walk into, a booker she can't email or an agent she can't pursue because of the presence of a problematic guy. We are all avoiding someone who could help us make money.

Louie used his power to feed a sickness inside of himself, and his actions affected the careers and lives of several extremely talented women. (As a woman who's worked with him, I was appalled by his behavior, yet also saddened by it, since he'd always been a champion for women by hiring them for multiple positions in his production company, and developing and writing two TV shows for female leads.) Many people are still disappointed with Louis's apology because he never actually wrote the words "I'm sorry." In August 2018, less than a year after he issued his statement, he made his foray back into stand-up. Though some believe he hasn't taken enough time off to process and atone for his transgressions, others are adamant that he should *never* be able to grace a comedy club stage again. But is that fair? If Louis had been a painter, musician, or photographer, he could still go on creating his art as a pariah. But in stand-up, there's no art without feedback; if there's no one to hear the jokes, stand-up doesn't exist. We comedians are vulnerable in a different way because we tend to bare our souls onstage, confessing secrets and sharing intimate stories about ourselves, our families, and our lives. It's the reason people in the audience believe that they genuinely know us.

But they don't. The comedian you see onstage is only a sliver of the person known to their family and friends. On May 30, 2017, a photo taken by noted and provocative photographer Tyler Shields was posted on TMZ. In the photo, Kathy Griffin is holding a Halloween mask of Donald Trump's head covered in ketchup. The image sparked outrage. The impromptu photo, taken at the end of the shoot, was in response to candidate Trump's misogynist comment about Megyn Kelly, the moderator of the first Republican presidential primary debate leading up to the 2016 election: "She gets out and she starts asking me all sorts of ridiculous questions. You could see there was blood coming out of her eyes, blood coming out of her wherever. In my opinion, she was off base."[2]

Some interpreted Trump's comments as a reference to menstruation, others as something else entirely. Many Americans agreed that his statement was inappropriate for a presidential candidate, but many others did not. Apparently, more people expect decorum from comedians than from a future "leader" of the free world.

We can argue whether the photo was repulsive and tasteless, and from the reaction, clearly it was to a substantial number of people, but the First Amendment clarifies that there's no question of Shields's and Griffin's right to create the photo. Though Griffin apologized, she was subsequently investigated by the FBI on suspicion of conspiracy to assassinate the president. She was also put on the No Fly List, fired by CNN, dropped from endorsement deals and by her representation, inundated with death threats, and had her upcoming comedy tour canceled. Griffin lay low in her home for a year, fearing for her life because of that photo. Was her intent to incite murder? Nope. It was a failed joke.

In 1991, Paul Reubens, a.k.a. Pee-wee Herman, was arrested in Florida during a random inspection of an X-rated movie theater. An officer claimed he'd witnessed Reubens masturbating during the film and took him into custody. Wait a minute! Weren't adult theaters created as "safe spaces" for jerking off to porn? See what I did there? (Thank God, in 2020 the number of arrests for indecent exposure in movie theaters is way down thanks to laptops, smartphones, and tablets, which allow people to view pornography in their own homes and SUVs, or in coffee shops, public libraries, airplanes, and on public transportation.) Pee-wee was a positive role model for children, and his show, *Pee-wee's Playhouse,* was a hit with kids and adults alike. So, naturally, the appropriate response to Reubens's conduct was to destroy his career. He became the butt of many jokes. Reubens pleaded no contest and used his required community service hours to fund and create two antidrug PSAs specifically produced for a child's comprehension level. What a perv!

Pee-wee Herman dressed in snug-fitting gray plaid suits, and I'll assume that Paul Reubens dressed in oversize pajamas during the time he was holed up at his friend Doris Duke's New Jersey estate after his arrest. I'll also assume that he received phone calls, watched TV news, and read newspaper articles detailing the cancellation of *Pee-wee's Playhouse* (which was running in syndication) and the removal of all Pee-wee kids' products from Toys"R"Us stores. This was before cell phones and the internet. Lucky him. Though many prominent stars voiced their support for Reubens, as did his undying fans, Pee-wee Herman became damaged goods because of the actions of Paul Reubens.

In 1997, Eddie Murphy was pulled over by the cops for picking up a person the Hollywood police called a "known transsexual prostitute." Her name was Atisone Seiuli, and there were outstanding warrants for her arrest. Murphy's publicist spun the story, saying that his client was a Good Samaritan for offering this poor and damaged soul a ride home. Murphy allegedly believed Seiuli was a biological woman who just happened to be hanging out in an area renowned for gay prostitution. The reason many people were so outraged was because Murphy's stand-up was widely considered to be homophobic. In his 1983 comedy special, he opens by saying, "I got some rules when I do my stand-up, I got rules and shit. Faggots aren't allowed to look at my ass while I'm onstage. That's why I keep moving while up here. You don't know where the faggot section is, you gotta keep moving, so if they do see it, quick, you switch, they don't get no long stares." He goes on to say that you can get AIDS from your wife if she kisses a gay guy. Not funny—especially during the AIDS crisis. (He did eventually apologize in 1996.)

After he was caught with Seiuli, Murphy's career stalled, and we didn't hear much from him for a while. An interesting note on this topic is that in Dave Chappelle's 2018 Netflix special, *Equanimity,* Chappelle talks about picking up a prostitute with beautiful breasts, only to find out later that she's a man. He admits to masturbating with her breasts because "technically, those fake titties were just as real as other fake titties in Los Angeles." Hilarious.

All of us make mistakes, have lapses in judgment, and do things we later regret. There is a plethora of stories about comedians' shitty, or even criminal, conduct to go around. Good comedians never ignore the elephant in the room. When a comedian gets on the stage and acknowledges his bad behavior, he appeases the audience's voyeuristic curiosity while mollifying their judgements about it, and subsequently owns the room. A controversial comic can charm and disarm with a couple of jokes. That's what I call power. In June 1980, after freebasing cocaine for a few days straight, Richard Pryor doused himself with 151-proof rum and set himself on fire. While still in flames, he ran down the street until he was subdued by the police. The odds that he would survive the incident were slim, but thankfully, he beat those odds. In his 1982 comedy special, *Live on the Sunset Strip,* Pryor brought that elephant right onstage with him. It's exactly what his fans wanted and needed.

Why me? Ten million motherfuckers freebasing, and I'm the one who blows up? When that fire hit your ass, it will sober your ass up quick!

I saw something, I went, "Well, that's a pretty blue. You know what? That looks like . . . FIRE!" Fire is inspirational. They should use it in the Olympics, because I ran the 100 in 4.3.

On September 5, 1991, during the MTV Video Music Awards, Paul Reubens entered to a standing ovation, walked to the podium, leaned down toward the microphone, and said, "Heard any good jokes lately?" The best! In 2018, Kathy Griffin came out of hiding by booking a fifteen-country tour of her show Laugh Your Head Off. She performed in beautiful theaters and got rave reviews, and though she was detained at every single airport, and to this day still cannot answer her own phone, she came home feeling somewhat vindicated. She continued to tour in North America, and when she announced that she'd be performing at Carnegie Hall, the show sold out within twenty-four hours! Laugh Your Head Off made Griffin millions of dollars. The previously low-profile Eddie Murphy is also enjoying a lucrative comeback, and when he hosted *SNL* in late 2019, he brought in the highest ratings for the show in more than two and a half years. I hadn't laughed like that in a long time.

As I write this, for most people, Louis C.K. has yet to satisfactorily acknowledge his elephant. Later in the evening on the day the news about him broke, I did a set at the Comedy Cellar, opening by saying, "Hey, everyone. Do you mind if I show you my penis?" The audience groaned, but like I always do, I continued, "What's wrong? At least I asked." Almost a year after Louis C.K. was outed, he did an unannounced set at the Cellar but didn't mention the scandal. Several days later, the Comedy Cellar's owner, my friend Noam Dworman, asked me to be a guest on the Cellar's podcast, *Live from the Table*. Jenna Amatulli from HuffPost was there to observe for a story she was writing about Louis's first set after the scandal.

In her story, Amatulli describes Noam as "The dad-type who interrupts you ten times at the dinner table after asking for your opinion on current events." Naturally I don't see him that way, since he's a teeny bit younger than me. But Noam is very smart, educated, talented, Jewy, and unabashedly opinionated. He exudes confidence, and as a club owner, he exercises his right to do whatever he desires in his space. His view of censorship is that if it is to be implemented, it "really needs a heavy justification." I agree. Very heavy. In addition, he makes the point that no one is forcing audience members to sit in a comedy club and listen to something that makes them uncomfortable. If they want to leave, they can—just don't make a scene, and you'll get a full refund.

When we were questioned by Amatulli about Louis's first set at the Comedy Cellar, nine months after his misconduct was made public, both Noam and I expressed frustration at his conspicuous lack of acknowledgment of the elephant in the room. How could a comic who was lauded for his brutal honesty onstage neglect to address something so glaringly obvious? I pointed out to Amatulli that "it was a missed opportunity. Acknowledge what's going on. Let's face it, he's been thinking about it for a long time. Everyone's been thinking, 'Is he going to talk about it?' That's the thing that I think really pissed people off. You just got onstage and didn't talk about it? Someone who talks about everything? It shows some sort of disconnect in my mind. Do you realize what happened?"

Louis has his own journey, and as he goes back to his stand-up roots, his act will undoubtedly be seen through a very different lens. A good number of his old fans will never forgive him, and his mere presence will trigger others. It's something he'll have to deal with for the rest of his life.

Right after more than fifty women accused Bill Cosby of sexual misconduct—and, in some cases, of allegedly drugging them first—I had a limo driver who insisted that there was no way it could be true. (Yes, I'd heard the rumors for years.) I told him that Dr. Huxtable didn't do it, Bill Cosby did. He responded like a lot of men: "Well, then why did those women wait so long to say something?" Ignorant, party of one, your table's ready.

Cliff Huxtable was a successful, funny, loving, smart, and sometimes embarrassing TV father. As such, he was an extremely important representation of the head of an African American family. He was the dad we've all, at least on occasion, dreamed of having. In the '80s, *The Cosby Show* was for many what *The Brady Bunch* was for me in the late '60s and early '70s—the family I aspired to have when I grew up. Bill Cosby's stand-up was also a big part of my youth, as was his animated show, *Fat Albert and the Cosby Kids*. Cosby's act was clean, funny, and the template for so many successful comedians who eventually became household names.

Offstage, Cosby berated poor black kids for wearing their pants too low. He went on tirades about African American adults having terrible grammar, squandering work and educational opportunities, and being terrible parents and role models. He also asked black men to stop beating their wives. And while he was publicly lambasting the community, privately, Mr. Cosby was slipping women roofies and raping them. He continued to do stand-up while his lawyers were preparing his "defense." Though eventually he was found guilty, he continues to deny all the allegations. Bill Cosby is no Cliff Huxtable—he's a hypocritical and arrogant rapist prick.

As I've said, the intimate nature of stand-up leads people to believe they know comedians personally. Yet as much as we thought we knew Mr. Cosby, we didn't, and as much as we thought we knew Louis C.K., we didn't. Through their stand-up, recordings, and TV shows, each of these men gave a voice to—and a reprieve from—our fears and anxieties. We identified with the parts of themselves they chose to share with us, which, in turn, validated our own feelings and view of the world. We quoted them and we idolized them for making our fraught lives funny. But the way I see it, Louis C.K. is not Bill Cosby. Louis is not in jail, nor does he deserve to be. As much as you try, you can't deny Louis's talent, you can't erase his body of work, and you can't stop him from doing stand-up, nor should you.

You also can't deny Cosby's body of work, even though it has all but disappeared from public view, and I'll never eat Jell-O pudding again without feeling violated, even if there's a dollop of whipped cream on top.

The Cosby Show is no longer streaming anywhere, though its positive message could have impacted generations to come. Cosby's current jokes are performed only for his prison guards and cellmates. For many, listening to Cosby's brilliant stand-up is a sad and painful reminder of who he really is.

Now, it's not my place to tell you which actions are inexcusable and which aren't, or even which comedians deserve a second chance and which don't. That's for you and your conscience to decide (though I do think our legal system's felony statutes provide a good starting point). I'm certain, however, that each of us is more than our worst action, and that forgiveness is in increasingly short supply in our tweet 'n' run world. Comedy is a democracy, a working democracy, where character matters. Banishing comedians means depriving us of laughter that heals, educates, and connects us. Banish wisely.

8

Comparing Apples to Orange Fuckface Presidents

As democracy is perfected, the office of president represents, more and more closely, the inner soul of the people. On some great and glorious day the plain folks of the land will reach their heart's desire at last and the White House will be adorned by a downright moron.

—H. L. MENCKEN

You can tell a lot about a person by what they find funny. I've never understood why some people laugh when they see someone trip on a sidewalk or fall off their bike or drive into the garage door by mistake. I always wondered what was so goddamn hilarious about seeing someone get hurt, watching property being destroyed, or terrifying someone. Am I missing something? Is it an acquired taste? Isn't it a bit sadistic? And please, whatever you do, don't confuse sadism with schadenfreude, because the latter can be delightful when it's a scumbag falling off a bike.

Have you ever seen Donald Trump laugh? Have you ever seen a photo or film of Adolf Hitler laughing? What about Vladimir Putin? Kim Jong-un? Mitch McConnell? Kellyanne Conway? Sarah Huckabee Sanders? Steve Bannon? Stephen Miller? You get the drift. Sure, there's footage of them smiling and chuckling, but their laughter always seems maniacal, like it's escaped from an evil place deep within them. You know the scenario: An upscale function, the rich and powerful mingling and sipping cocktails, the camera pans the room, stopping on the mob boss (or the mad scientist, or the ruthless general), their face angled down as some unctuous sycophant whispers into their ear. A moment later you see them guffaw. I can assure you that whatever's being whispered doesn't start with "knock-knock." I can promise you that they're laughing at someone else's expense or misfortunes. I can give you a guarantee that they are not laughing at themselves.

Except for former senator Al Franken; Volodymyr Zelensky, the president of Ukraine; and Jón Gnarr, the former mayor of Reykjavík, I'm not aware of any other comedians who've become politicians. Basically, for any comic, going into politics would mean the end of their professional stand-up career.

There have been, however, some comedians who've mounted faux presidential campaigns. In 1928, Will Rogers ran as the nominee of the Anti-Bunk Party. The candidate's one promise: if elected, he would resign. Comedian Pat Paulsen made his first run at the Oval Office in 1968, representing the S.T.A.G. (Straight Talking American Government) Party. Paulsen's campaign was a combination of political satire, silliness, and feigned indifference. He maintained, "We have nothing to fear but fear itself . . . and, of course, the boogieman," and addressed voters' concerns, rhetorically asking them, "Will I solve our civil rights problems? Will I unite this country and bring it forward? Will I obliterate the national debt? Sure, why not?" Paulsen would run for president five more times, actually garnering thousands of votes from Americans tired of politics as usual. And in 1940, Gracie Allen, who performed with her husband, George Burns, as the comedy duo Burns and Allen, made her bid for the country's highest office heading the ticket of the Surprise Party. Regarding the selection of a vice-presidential running mate, Allen replied that she would not tolerate vice in her administration. In October 2008, Stephen Colbert announced that he would run for both the Republican and Democratic nominations for president, until he found out the fee to enter the Republican primary was $35,000, as opposed to $2,500 for the Democratic primary. His slogan was "First to secede, first to succeed!" He dropped out on November 5.

I can't think of a politician turned stand-up (but if that were to happen, I know who'd kill it as a comedian—Barack Obama). Comedians make jokes and government officials make decisions that have profound effects on the lives of thousands—often millions—of people. The only power comedians have is our voices. We encourage people to think about how what happens in the world affects each and every one of us differently. That ultimately brings people together. Spewing offensive and danger-ous lies from the Oval Office without irony or humor does just the opposite—and because of the disproportionate power of large corporations and the wealthy, Trump and his ilk frequently aren't even speaking to the audience directly in front of them. A come-dian is one with her audience.

It's crucial to understand when speech constitutes a threat. One can determine this from the source. When the speech comes from a powerful political operative, it's dangerous and can even be deadly. When it comes from a comedian, it's a fucking joke. As previously pointed out, political humor is important and often a fun way of getting information out to many people.

The most important function of political satire is to shed light on abuse, incompetence, hypocrisy, and misuse of power. Throughout our country's history, comedians have taken on our presidents' characters and policies. In 1927, after the Great Missis-sippi Flood left parts of the South under thirty feet of water, Will Rogers joked that limited-government hawk Calvin Coolidge had been slow to respond to the calamity out of a "hope that those needing relief will perhaps have conveniently died in the mean-time." Some other examples:

BOB HOPE (1967)

President Johnson couldn't be here tonight. He's busy. He's placing a wreath on the tomb of the "unknown foreign policy."

JOHNNY CARSON (1973)

Did you know Richard Nixon is the only president whose formal portrait was painted by a police sketch artist?

MORT SAHL (1980)

Reagan won because he ran against Jimmy Carter. If he'd run unopposed, he would have lost.

DENNIS MILLER (1991)

Now let me get this straight. Bush is anti-abortion, but pro–death penalty. I guess it's all in the timing, huh?

DAVID LETTERMAN (1998)

No move ever goes smoothly. Today Clinton's brand-new desk arrived. He had to send it back, apparently not enough head room.

ME AGAIN (2000)

I performed at a Democratic fund-raiser in Miami Beach a couple of years ago, and I performed for Bill Clinton. I did stand-up comedy for him as well.

MARGARET CHO (2003)

George Bush is not Hitler. He would be if he fucking applied himself.

CONAN O'BRIEN (2012)

Tonight, President Obama and Mitt Romney debate foreign policy. Pundits say it will be close, but it will probably go to the candidate who wore the "I killed Osama bin Laden" T-shirt.

Most occupants of the White House have taken it in stride, accepting that it's just one unfortunate part of their job.

Political comedy is especially important in the Trump era because freedom of speech—one of the most important powers that the US Constitution guarantees to the people—is being hampered by the president's disrespect for the document, the opaqueness of his administration, the Supreme Court's decision in *Citizens United v. Federal Election Commission,* and the way money has supplanted the voice of the citizenry in determining the priorities of our elected representatives. And please, do not underestimate the influence of years of daytime trash TV, "reality" television, and the more recent impact of social media in polluting the standards of character and intelligence in our elected officials. At this point, nothing is shocking or sacred. You can be an accused child molester running for a Senate seat in Alabama and still get the support of the president of the United States. The shit that comes out of Trump's mouth would get any other person suspended from school, kicked out of the house, or fired. It appears that, today, people find nobody more dangerous than a comedian telling a joke.

On *The Late Show with Stephen Colbert,* the host mocked Trump's dismissal of respected journalist John Dickerson during an interview on *Face the Nation.* During the interview, Trump literally refused to face the nation when given the opportunity to explain exactly what he meant in a recent tweet implying that

President Obama had wiretapped him. Trump also obnoxiously mentioned to Dickerson that he refers to the show as "Deface the Nation." (FYI—there is no way he thought of that himself.)

Colbert's bit on this was:

> John Dickerson is a fair-minded journalist, and one of the most competent people who will ever walk into your office, and you treat him like that. Mr. President, you're not the POTUS, you're the "gloat-us." You're the glutton with the button. You're a regular "Gorge Washington." You're the "presi-dunce," but you're turning into a real "prick-tator." Sir, you attract more skinheads than free Rogaine. You have more people marching against you than cancer. You talk like a sign language gorilla that got hit in the head. In fact, the only thing your mouth is good for is being Vladimir Putin's cock holster.

Colbert got a lot of blowback (pun intended) for the "cock holster" remark. It was deemed vulgar and homophobic. Okay, I'm a gay, and I'm telling you right now that it wasn't homophobic. And since when did the right-wing media become so concerned with the way gay people feel? It's really heartwarming to know how concerned they are about us—that is, outside of our gay conversion-therapy classes. People called on CBS to fire Colbert, rallied the public to boycott the show, and urged the show's sponsors to pull their support. There were harsh editorials, angry tweets, and complaints to the FCC. I can't imagine what would've happened to Colbert if he'd said that he likes to grab a woman by the pussy and just start kissing her without asking.

Colbert ended up apologizing—if you need to call it that—and it happened to be quite awesome:

Now, if you saw my monologue Monday, you know that I
was a little upset at Donald Trump for insulting a friend
of mine. So, at the end of that monologue, I had a few
choice insults for the president in return. I don't regret
that. He, I believe, can take care of himself. I have jokes, he
has the launch codes. So it's a fair fight.

That night, Colbert had Jon Stewart (who happens to be one
of the show's executive producers) on as a guest. Stewart echoed
Colbert's comments, saying to his friend:

The things that you say, even if they're crass, or even if
they, in some ways, are not respectful enough to the
office of the presidency— We can insult. He can injure. It's
the difference between insult and injury. For the life of
me, I do not understand why in this country we try to hold
comedians to a standard we do not hold leaders to. It's
bizarre.

It's beyond bizarre, Jon. It's fucking terrifying.

I appeared on *The Late Show* in 2017 and remarked to Colbert that "Trump's the only native New Yorker who's never been
in therapy *and* he's the New Yorker who needs it the most." His
tawdry behavior has forced seasoned journalists to utter words
and phrases that were previously unthinkable on network television. Watching NBC's respected anchor Andrea Mitchell try to
repeat Trump's disparaging comments about immigrants coming
from "shithole countries" without actually saying "shithole" really hit home with me. Trump continually says and tweets racist,
misogynistic, Islamophobic, and juvenile things. He blatantly lies.

He attaches nasty epithets to the names of his adversaries: sleepy, little, low-IQ, crooked, lyin', fat, crazy, wacky, sleazy, leaking, Pocahontas—the list goes on and on. And guess what? Not one of those names are funny. In an article by Meri Wallace, LCSW, in *Psychology Today,* she explains, "It is helpful to know that name-calling is part of a preschooler's natural development."[1] Let this sink in: the president of the United States of America literally behaves like a toddler. Now *that's* fucked up.

In June 2017, after forty-nine people at Pulse nightclub in Orlando, Florida, were massacred in the deadliest attack on the LGBTQ community in US history, instead of extending at least the standard lame and infuriating "thoughts and prayers" to the victims and their families, Trump, oblivious to anyone but Trump, took the tragedy as an opportunity for self-aggrandizement, tweeting, "Appreciate the congrats for being right on radical Islamic terrorism." He called for a "total and complete shutdown of Muslims entering the United States until our country's representatives can figure out what is going on." At his presidential announcement speech, he stated that

> When Mexico sends its people, they're not sending their best. They're not sending you. They're not sending you. They're sending people that have lots of problems, and they're bringing those problems with us. They're bringing drugs. They're bringing crime. They're rapists. And some, I assume are good people.

In regard to the late senator and war hero John McCain, Trump, the five-time deferred draft dodger, said, "I like heroes who weren't captured." This is how he unapologetically speaks.

Let's just focus for a moment on how Trump's speech affects not only the office of the presidency, but all of America's constituents. When I was a child, regardless of political leanings, people respected the commander in chief. After all, he represents us and our enviable democracy to people all over the globe. His and his wife's preferences in clothing, food, music, and art often set the trends of the time. It's the president's behavior that models the norm for young people. Honestly, I've never seen people acting more callous, rude, and petty than they have during Trump's term so far. The president of the United States is supposed to actualize the laudable values that made our country an example to the world. He has power—enormous power. He has the power to act on the repugnant shit that comes out of his mouth and fingers. He appoints judges inclined to void voting rights and protections for people of color. He champions legislation that controls women's bodies. He issues executive orders revoking the right of trans people to serve in our military. He guts environmental protections, harming us and condemning our children and grandchildren to a future on an inhospitable and dangerous planet. He siphons funds from lifesaving programs Americans depend on and funnels that money into a ridiculous and unnecessary wall to feed his ego. Most egregious of all, he denies the grave threat to our voting systems. Your vote, the elemental representation of free speech, may be weakened or rendered moot by this president's refusal to protect our elections from foreign and domestic interference. None of this is funny. And just as comedians aren't the president, THIS president, despite the laughs (of the wickedly maniacal kind) he elicits at the rallies of his minions, is NOT a comedian.

Overall, with presidents, it's a good sign if he—or, someday soon, she (God willing)—is funny. But to be funny, you have to be smart. You have to understand nuance. You have to possess a vocabulary composed of more than thirty words that you recycle endlessly. Most important, you have to have emotional intelligence. This explains why, despite being a self-proclaimed "stable genius" who has "the best words," Trump is about as funny as being forced to carry your rapist's baby to term.

Here are a few quips by former presidents who had decent senses of humor.

ANDREW JOHNSON

Washington, D.C., is twelve square miles bordered by reality.

ABRAHAM LINCOLN

If I were two-faced, would I be wearing this one?

HERBERT HOOVER

Blessed are the young, for they shall inherit the national debt.

JOHN F. KENNEDY

I was almost late here today, but I had a very good taxi driver who brought me through the traffic jam. I was going to give him a very large tip and tell him to vote Democratic and then I remember some advice Senator Green had given me, so I gave him no tip at all and told him to vote Republican.

GEORGE W. BUSH

No matter how tough it gets, I have no intention of becoming a lame-duck president. Unless, of course, Cheney accidentally shoots me in the leg.

BARACK OBAMA

> Some folks still don't think I spend enough time with
> Congress. "Why don't you get a drink with Mitch
> McConnell?" they ask. Really? Why don't YOU get a drink
> with Mitch McConnell?

Unfortunately for the country, Trump, like most humorless people, has no idea when other people are being funny. Those who are comedically challenged not only have a hard time understanding jokes, but they're also unable to appreciate the humor in things—especially in themselves. When someone makes a good joke about me, not only do I laugh, I'm hugely flattered. People like Trump take jokes about themselves as attacks, and since they're incapable of responding with a clever witticism of their own, they try to dismiss the jokes as unfunny. Then they use their power to label the comedians who tell those jokes as losers or talentless. Sad!

Trump was in attendance when Seth Meyers hosted the 2011 White House Correspondents' Dinner. If you go online and watch a clip, you'll clearly see Trump's inability to laugh at himself when Meyers makes jokes about him. Trump looks angry and full of vengeance. He's been attacking Meyers ever since, insulting him on Twitter regularly. And you can bet your ass that Meyers continues to poke fun at Trump—because, again, that's what comedians are supposed to do.

Trump's been too thin-skinned to attend the White House Correspondents' Dinner during his reign—I mean, presidency. Of course, that didn't stop comics Hasan Minhaj and Michelle Wolf, who performed at the dinner in 2017 and 2018, respectively, from telling jokes to power:

HASAN MINHAJ

Now, a lot of people in the media say that Donald Trump goes golfing too much. You guys are always like, "He goes golfing too much," which raises a very important question: Why do you care? Do you want to know what he is doing when he's golfing? Being president. Let the man Putt-Putt. Keep him distracted. Teach him how to play badminton. Tell him he has a great body for bobsledding. Play him tic-tac-toe. The longer you keep him distracted, the longer we are not at war with North Korea. Every time he goes golfing, the headline should read: Trump golfing. Apocalypse delayed.

MICHELLE WOLF

Here we are, the White House Correspondents' Dinner. Like a porn star says when she's about to have sex with a Trump, "Let's get this over with."

⎯

Of course, Trump isn't here—if you haven't noticed, he's not here. And I know, I know, I would drag him here myself, but it turns out the president of the United States is the one pussy you're not allowed to grab.

⎯

I'm going to try a fun new thing, okay? I'm going to say, "Trump is so broke," and you guys go, "How broke is he?" All right?

Trump is so broke, he has to fly failed business class.

Trump is so broke, he looked for foreign oil in Don Jr.'s hair.

Trump is so broke, he had to borrow money from the Russians and now he's compromised and susceptible to blackmail and possibly responsible for the collapse of the Republic. Yay, it's a fun game!

After Wolf's performance, Trump predictably maligned her material and her abilities as a comedian. That's no surprise. In 2011, when Trump agreed to be roasted on Comedy Central, one of the conditions he placed on his appearance was that there be no jokes about the size of his bank account. Wolf unabashedly mocked his personal worth, both monetarily and emotionally. The Donald took this as yet another opportunity to insult Seth Meyers:

> 10:38 PM Apr 29, 2018 @realDonaldTrump
> The White House Correspondents' Dinner was a failure last year, but this year was an embarrassment to everyone associated with it. The filthy "comedian" totally bombed (couldn't even deliver her lines-much like the Seth Meyers weak performance). Put Dinner to rest, or start over!

Since funny retorts take a modicum of intelligence and self-awareness, and Trump's humor IQ is smaller than his glove size, his responses always have an air of "I know you are, but what am I?" This is standard for him. The only mildly funny thing about his response is that the man who popularized the phrases "shit-hole countries" and "grab 'em by the pussy" is calling someone else filthy.

You may be wondering why it matters so much that Trump can't take a joke, or why it's a big deal that he lashes out at comedians. As I've pointed out before, jokes humanize you—especially those in which you acknowledge a flaw or weak spot in yourself that other people are aware of. When you laugh at your own expense and allow others to laugh with you, you shed your armor, and their trepidation toward you dissolves. A wannabe autocrat can only get away with saying and doing outrageous things by fostering fear. The steadfastness of Trump loyalists depends on his ability to fearmonger. And until he's consolidated enough power to instill fear all by himself, he needs scapegoats to keep people afraid: afraid of immigrants taking their jobs, afraid of Democrats in power taking away their guns, afraid of LGBTQ people destroying their freedom of religion, afraid of Muslims wanting to institute Sharia law and committing acts of terrorism, afraid of Jews replacing them (please, we're only 2 percent of the population), afraid of minorities bleeding social welfare programs dry. Autocrats like Vladimir Putin and Kim Jong-un remain in power because people are terrified of them (for good reason), and it's obvious that Trump aspires to be just like them.

It may seem like I'm spending too many pages on Trump. Believe me when I say that I wish I didn't have to, but it's necessary. Democracy is fragile, and Trump has mounted an all-out assault on America's values, its traditions, and its Constitution. As time has distanced us from the threats of Nazism, fascism, and communism, here in the US, political opponents and their supporters have increasingly been hurling insults like "Nazi" and "fascist" at officials and policies they don't agree with while not really understanding the words' horrific histories. Indeed, comparisons to the evils of the Soviet Union or the Third Reich have become, for too many people, little more than a way to describe anything distasteful. Now, at this point in time, when we find ourselves with a president who seems to be using *The Dictator's Handbook* as a guide to governing the country, many Americans have become desensitized and don't recognize the danger. We've become, literally, "The Country Who Cried Hitler."

Yes, this is a book about comedy, but during Hitler's rise in Germany, comedians were among the first to call attention to what was really going on. Jokes and laughter about Hitler and the Third Reich weakened Nazi propaganda. Hitler despised being laughed at, so he attacked the comedians, cartoonists, and cabaret performers who mocked him. How did he do it? By passing the Treachery Act of 1934. Under the law, telling anti-Nazi jokes or listening to them were considered acts of treason, punishable by imprisonment or death. Yes, death. I mean, there have been times I've died onstage, but I woke up the next morning and went on with my life. Going to prison for a joke seems so over the top. "So, what're you in for?" "Funny you should ask . . . Mike Pence and Lindsey Graham walk into a bathhouse . . ."

In an interview I did with Ira Glasser, a former executive director of the American Civil Liberties Union (ACLU), Glasser explained that:

> What happened to Germany in the thirties wasn't because they had an independent federal court system and a first amendment. It happened because they *didn't* have those things, and so people in power had power that was not limited by rights—I mean all rights. Something else I find most people don't understand and haven't thought about is that liberty and democracy are not the same thing. Democracy basically means the rule—the majority governs by some system of votes and elections—and liberty means the majority doesn't get to govern everything. That just because there are more whites than blacks, whites cannot

> pass a law denying blacks rights. And [just because] men
> have more power than women, men can't deny women
> the right to vote. I use the right to vote because, in fact,
> for most of our history, that is precisely what men did with
> women and precisely what whites did with blacks.

Power has always been a crucial component when it comes to free speech in our country. Without free speech, lives are lost. In the early 1980s, AIDS started to infiltrate the LGBT community. Men could no longer hide their sexuality; they were wasting away before our eyes. They walked down the street with sores on their bodies, so thin that, physically, they were a fraction of who they once were. My friends and I signed up as volunteer workers at the very first AIDS Walk New York and continued to do it for years. In my free time, I volunteered at God's Love We Deliver, an organization that provides hot meals to homebound people unable to shop and cook for themselves. As a whole, the community felt overwhelmed emotionally and financially, and President Ronald Reagan and his lovely large-headed wife were far from helpful. Ronnie wouldn't even utter the term *AIDS* publicly until he was well into his second term. By then over ten thousand Americans had died from HIV/AIDS and even more were infected with the virus. His communications director, the revolting Pat Buchanan, proclaimed that AIDS was "nature's revenge on gay men." Yup, he's allowed to say that, but God forbid a comic tells an off-color joke on television.

During a 1982 press conference held by Reagan's press secretary, Larry Speakes, the journalist Lester Kinsolving was the first to question Speakes on the topic of AIDS. It should be noted that later on, Kinsolving, due to his religious beliefs, was very outspoken about his opposition to gay rights organizations. This gives you some idea of how LGBT people were spoken of at the time, and also the reason people stayed in the closet.

> LESTER KINSOLVING: Does the president have any reaction to the announcement by the Centers for Disease Control in Atlanta that AIDS is now an epidemic in over six hundred cases?
>
> LARRY SPEAKES: AIDS? I haven't got anything on it.
>
> KINSOLVING: Over a third of them have died. It's known as "gay plague." [*press pool laughter*] No, it is. It's a pretty serious thing. One in every three people that get this have died. And I wonder if the president was aware of this.
>
> SPEAKES: I don't have it. [*press pool laughter*] Do you?
>
> KINSOLVING: You don't have it? Well, I'm relieved to hear that, Larry! [*press pool laughter*]
>
> SPEAKES: Do you?
>
> KINSOLVING: No, I don't.
>
> SPEAKES: You didn't answer my question. How do you know? [*press pool laughter*]
>
> KINSOLVING: Does the president—in other words, the White House—look on this as a great joke?
>
> SPEAKES: No, I don't know anything about it, Lester.[2]

Later exchanges include more joking and apathy about AIDS, including from other members of the press, even after more was known about the seriousness of the epidemic.

I was in my twenties, and my friends were dying. That's not supposed to happen. AIDS was the gay Vietnam. It forced movie star Rock Hudson, a close friend of Nancy Reagan, to come out of the closet. It had originally been reported that he had liver cancer. He traveled to Paris to seek treatment that he couldn't get in the USA. Dominique Dormant, a French army doctor who'd previously treated Hudson, needed to get the actor into a French military hospital, which, at the time, was the only place in the world that had the capability to treat him. Hudson couldn't be admitted to that hospital because the commanding officer refused. In a last-ditch effort, he called on the First Lady because he had been close friends with the Reagans for a long time. And guess what? She refused. She fucking said no! I knew she said no to drugs, but to deny help to her good friend who's dying of AIDS? That's what I call a cunty move. This gay disease was all the excuse the haters needed in order to trumpet their superior heterosexuality.

In the summer of 1984, the president of American Airlines opened a breakfast at the Republican National Convention by joking that "gay" stood for "got AIDS yet?" HA! HA! HA! So funny! OMG! My stomach hurts! And you know what? All those evil fucks probably guffawed. This behavior, and the fact that Reagan decreased funding for AIDS research at one of the most critical moments of the crisis, galvanized our community into action. This was life or death for us. We had to find a way to stop gay men and drug users from dying. We had a common purpose. No more being quiet. Silence = Death.

In 1932, Will Rogers said, "Everything is changing. Now people are taking their comedians seriously and the politicians as a joke, when it used to be vice versa."[3] Oh, how true that rings today. In December 2003, I was invited to perform at a fund-raiser for presidential candidate Howard Dean. I wasn't a particularly huge fan of Dean, but he was leading in the polls at the time, and I was going to support anyone who could get Bush and Cheney out of office. It was a pretty cool event—a bunch of comics doing sets at a party space in Chelsea in New York City. Janeane Garofalo, David Cross, Kate Clinton, myself, and a couple of other performers were there. As with all special events, the show started late. I think I had a glass of wine, which I NEVER do before I get onstage, but I wasn't doing more than ten minutes and I'd been noshing throughout the evening.

The audience was a diverse group of Democrats who were incredibly pissed off about the Iraq War, which was based on false intelligence about Saddam Hussein having weapons of mass destruction. Not to mention they were also fed up with every other one of Bush's policies. To us, George W. Bush, Dick Cheney, and Secretary of Defense Donald Rumsfeld were the axis of evil. You might have noticed that many people seem to have forgotten how miserable we were during the Bush years because we never, even under the heaviest drug-induced psychosis, could ever have envisioned the evil clown in the White House today. Cheney and Rumsfeld are still evil, but George W. now spends his time relaxing, painting, and flirting with Michelle Obama at state funerals. His wife, Laura, and his daughters, Jenna and Barbara, have come out as supporters of LGBTQ equality and a woman's right to choose, and his late father, George H. W. Bush, officiated at a same-sex wedding in 2013. So, people change. Well, some people do.

By the time I got onstage that night, the audience was fired up. All of us were being very political and getting really big laughs. At that time, I used to open my set with this joke: "I live on the Upper West Side of Manhattan, and the strangest thing happened to me today. I was walking down the street and I saw this Asian baby WITH Asian parents." It was a nice icebreaker for New York audiences. Another joke I did, which is still a favorite of Jews everywhere, was about Senator Joe Lieberman, who was also running for president on the Democratic ticket:

Joseph Lieberman is running for president, and he's an Orthodox Jew, which is going to be a big problem if he becomes the nominee. Think about it, the heat of the campaign is in the fall, which also happens to be Jew season. Can you imagine his answering machine message during that time period? [*in my Jewish-mother voice*] "Hi. You've reached the office of Joseph Lieberman. Our office hours are Monday through Thursday from eight A.M. to six P.M. and on Fridays from sunrise to sunset. We will be closed September twenty-fourth through the twenty-sixth for the festival of Rosh Hashanah, we will be closed October third for Yom Kippur, we will be closed October ninth to the fifteenth for Sukkot, we will be closed October sixteenth and seventeenth for Shemini Atzeret and Simchat Torah. We will reopen on Monday, October twentieth. Thank you for calling, and SHALOM!!!"

I also did a joke about how Lieberman's wife's name is Hadassah, which isn't her real name. Her original name was CHHHHHHHHHHHH, but that was too Jewish, so they changed it to Hadassah. I went on to do a joke about how Dick Cheney talks like Mary Jo Buttafuoco. I use that reference for anyone who talks out of the side of their mouth. Currently, it's Sarah Fuckabee Sanders. Anyway, I was so riled up that at the end of my set, I said right into the microphone, "Just remember! We have to get that living, breathing piece of shit out of office!! Good night, everyone!!" Not the most eloquent choice of words to describe the leader of the free world, nor my finest moment, I'll admit, but I felt empowered, and I tend to have no edit button whatsoever. Little did I know that Howard Dean was there listening and getting very pissed off, not just at me, but at the other comics who were all being subversive, irreverent, truthful, and very funny. There was also a lot of press there.

The following day, everything blew up. The *New York Post* ran an article headlined "HOWARD'S HATEFEST," and yes, it was in ALL CAPS. The article was written by conservative journalist Deborah Orin, who's since passed away. Here's a summary (along with my comments).

Orin reported that all the comedians had been vying to see who could cram the most F-words into a single sentence. (Yes, we had a huge competition. The winner got fucked after the show.) Then she singled out my use of the phrase "piece of living, breathing s——." (Oh, Deborah, it's "living, breathing piece of SHIT!" Everyone knows that "piece of" ALWAYS comes before the word "shit.") She went on to claim that there was "something to offend everyone" (I'm so glad you got that) and that Joe Lieberman, just because he's Orthodox, was ridiculed for missing too many perfectly good campaigning days due to the number of Jewish holidays. (Yes, I ridiculed HIM, but it had nothing to do with making people laugh about how many Jewish holidays there are. Mocking him was my entire objective. Right on, sister!) Orin also called out Kate Clinton for referring to Dick Cheney's wife, Lynne, as "Lon Chaney," and for saying that Cheney's daughter Mary was a "big lezzie." (Okay, here I take umbrage at Orin's supercilious tone. Fuck you, Deb! That's hilarious. Lon Chaney became a star for playing ghouls, and WHO is more ghoulish than Lynne Cheney? And it's not like Kate outed Mary. Her hair did that first.)

"Even the apolitical 'jokes' were ugly," Orin complained, "like a suggestion that it's bizarre to see an Asian baby with Asian parents because so many Asian babies are adopted by whites." (That explanation of the joke made it even more hilarious. Great work!) As she began wrapping up, Orin told readers that while

Dean noted, "I just don't have much tolerance for ethnic humor" and that some of the comedians' language was "wrong," he said nothing about the X-rated attacks on Bush and the Cheneys. (He didn't? WHAT?!?! That's awful. I can't believe he didn't refer to those filthy attacks—especially the one about anal.)

In concluding her take on the evening, Orin described the tone of the event as a left-wing version of a Ku Klux Klan meeting and cited a remark by Rep. Peter King (R-NY): "If some Southern redneck talked like this about a liberal, everyone would denounce it. But because it's Upper West Side humor, somehow it's supposed to be chic." (Chic? Like a trendy hat or a pair of eyeglasses? Do I sense a bit of envy? And this from a man who equated football players kneeling during the national anthem with the Nazi salute and described people from Japan as "Japs" on national television?)

After this article appeared in the *Post*, other newspapers, local and national, picked up the story. The AP picked it up, CNN broadcast about it, and people were writing op-eds based on limited and out-of-context information. This was before Facebook and Twitter, so I suppose I was lucky. Readers digesting and believing someone else's completely subjective opinion about comedy material is very dangerous to performers. I got hate mail. I got death threats. Someone wrote to me, "We're not responsible for what happens to you or your family." I was so fucking terrified. My webmaster called me to say that they were going to shut down my server for a few days. And for some reason, every time I took a flight for the next few years, I was "randomly selected" for a pat down. Here I am, I've never committed a crime, I don't own a gun, I just have a filthy mouth (as my mother used to love to say), and I'm being targeted by Homeland Security. What is wrong with this picture?

This experience changed me a lot. Never before had my life or my kids' lives been threatened because of something I said onstage. Reading the subjective, one-sided article made me even more invested in the fight for freedom of speech. Comedians shouldn't be vilified because they use words you don't approve of or because you don't agree with their political leanings. I doubt that when they composed the Bill of Rights the Founders were thinking about some poor schlubby stand-up comic making twenty-five bucks on a Tuesday night in some basement with a mic. I am sure, however, that if they had been thinking about schlubby comedians, they would have written the First Amendment to protect them.

In 2013, North Korean comedian Lee Choon Hong was arrested during her act and sent away to do hard labor in a coal mine. Hard labor because of a slip of the tongue that was displeasing to the government?! In 2014, Egyptian comedian Bassem Youssef was forced to flee his country because of jokes he had made about the government. As comics, we're damn lucky we live in the USA, but it does seem like times are changing.

I recently spoke to the comedian Ahmed Ahmed about one of the most ludicrous things to ever happen to a stand-up comic. You're not going to believe this one. Actually, with today's climate, you probably will.

Ahmed Ahmed was born in Helwan, Egypt. A month after he was born, his family immigrated to the United States and settled in Riverside, California, halfway between Los Angeles and Palm Springs. In 1989, when he was nineteen, Ahmed moved to Hollywood to pursue acting, where he made a great living playing terrorists and cabdrivers. (If only there were more stereotypical roles for tall Jewish lesbians!) He started doing comedy in '94, and after Mitzi Shore "passed" him at The Comedy Store in '99, officially adding him to the club's roster of performers, he moved his main focus to stand-up.

On May 11, 2019, Ahmed was working at Off The Hook Comedy Club in Naples, Florida. Most comedy clubs have terrible names, but for this story, "Off The Hook" was prescient. Ahmed opened his set by asking, "How many Middle Eastern people do we have in the audience? Clap if you're from the Middle East." (FYI, immediately acknowledging something the audience is going to focus on right away is a perfect way for a comedian to start a set. Addressing whatever it is on your own terms allows you to own it while disarming the crowd at the same time.) A few members of the audience clapped, and in response, Ahmed said, "All right. We've got a handful of us in here, nice. But hey, it only takes one of us [*pause*] to tell a joke. But seriously, lock the doors." It was during that one- to two-second pause when all the trouble began.

Apparently during that pause, a man in the audience felt threatened, or should I say triggered?

After the show, Ahmed did the same thing he always does. He stood at the exit to shake hands and take photos with the audience—it's called a meet and greet. After that, he went home. At about 6:40 P.M. the following day, Ahmed was sitting at a table in the club going over his notes, when the manager walked over to tell him that two police officers wanted to speak to him. The officers started by saying that they were sorry, but they had to respond to a call the police department had received from a man who said he'd feared for his life at Ahmed's show the previous night.

Here's a portion of that call, with some side notes from me:

CALLER (LET'S REFER TO HIM AS "RACIST ASSHOLE"—IT'S MUCH MORE PERSONAL): There was a comedian . . . he's um . . . his name is Ahmed Ahmed . . . and he's um . . . . . . you know, Middle Eastern.

(Oooooooo!)

OPERATOR: Uh-huh.

RACIST ASSHOLE: And first thing he said when he got out on the stage was, "Okay, how many Middle Eastern people do we have here?" And a whole bunch of people raised their hands.

O: Uh-huh.

RA: I guess they went to see him because he was Middle Eastern.

(Yeah, that's exactly why they went to see him. In fact, my entire audience is always filled with people who share the same genetic makeup as me.)

O: Uh-huh.

RA: You know, when you hear the name Ahmed Ahmed . . .

(Actually, I don't know.)

I went because I get free tickets.

(Fuck you, you cheap piece of shit.)

O: Okay.

RA: And as the people raised their hands, he said, "Where are you from?" "Oh, I'm from Iraq," "I'm from Iran," "I'm from Pakistan," "I'm from here," "I'm from there." He said, "That's great!" He said, "We can organize our own little terrorist organization."

(WHAT?!?)

Racist Asshole went on to say that he was really bothered by that, so he yelled out, "YEAH! The paddy wagon's going to be outside to get all of you." (Great heckle, jerk-off!) And then, referring to Ahmed's joke, he asked the operator, "Is that something that, ah, should not be said?" (Lemme answer that for you, dickwad: NO! He can say whatever the fuck he wants to say. He's a comedian in a comedy club! And if he was a cashier in a supermarket, a chef in a restaurant, or a quality-control guy at a catheter factory, he could say it there, too!)

I'm pretty sure this is who Hillary Clinton was referring to when she mentioned that "basket of deplorables." Things are absolutely out of control! He called the fucking police to report a joke he didn't like! We live in AMERICA!

The police officers were just as dismayed by the situation as Ahmed was. They were even laughing about it a bit. Before leaving, one of the officers told Ahmed, "Don't change your material. Keep doing what you're doing."

The operator who took the call left a message for Ahmed, apologizing that she had sent the police out, but explaining that when someone calls with a concern, she has to address it.

"I was thinking, 'Oh boy, Naples—this is not a good look,'" she said, adding that she thought the caller was probably struggling with the fact that, as he told his story, he realized he was a racist, and he probably hadn't thought that about himself before then. And, she pointed out, since he phoned the non-emergency line so as not to tie up a 911 operator, he must have known, on some level, that his complaint was nonsensical. Ahmed was a true gentleman through all of this. He took advantage of the press he was getting, and some of the statements he made about what happened were not only funny but thought-provoking: "Terrorists don't do meet and greets! We don't say, 'Death to America!' and

then, 'But wait, let's do selfies first.'" Exactly!!! I'm not sure terrorists even have a sense of humor. I can't imagine one of them
watching *Napoleon Dynamite,* then strapping on explosives and
blowing himself up in a crowded bazaar just for laughs. During
his press appearances, Ahmed offered Racist Asshole free tickets
to another show—along with a hug—but of course, the coward
remains anonymous.

How is it that in our country, a haven of freedom and opportunity to which immigrants have flocked for over two hundred
years, a person could feel so threatened by a comedian telling a
joke that he thinks it warrants a call to the police? I'll tell you
how. Because people in power are abusing the First Amendment
by spreading hate and lies. And those who believe what they're
being told grow fearful, are easily triggered, and react in ways
they believe to be patriotic. We don't live in a dictatorship . . . yet.
But if this behavior continues, we're going to be in bigger trouble
than we ever imagined.

Another thing I believe is worth mentioning is that both of
the police officers dispatched to the club were people of color (and
one was female). I hate to say it, but I'm not so certain that things
would have gone as smoothly for Ahmed if two white male officers had shown up. This is just a symptom of a much bigger
problem, and it's not going away.

A couple of years ago, Ahmed moved to Malaysia. When I
asked him why, he gave me a few reasons, not the least of which
was the rising level of Islamophobia in the US. As I mentioned,
when Ahmed was a month old, his family came to the US for a
better life. It's too bad Ahmed needed to move elsewhere to find it.

When I asked Ira Glasser why the climate has changed so
much for comics, he told me:

Power still prevails. It takes decades, if not centuries, for the enforceable law to catch up with the law the way it's written. And the difference between comedians and Trump is that he has power and you don't. And that's why people who are powerless are discriminated against and oppressed—whether they're comedians or blacks or Latinos or women or gays or American Indians or Jews or whatever—when you're in the minority, you can never outvote the majority. And you're doing things that are unpopular, which is to say, going to agitate the majority. You're the ones who have the most interest in preventing that majority from deciding whose speech to prohibit.

In 2019, the White House Correspondents' Association seemingly gave in to the Crybaby in Chief and decided not to feature a comedian roasting the room and the president at their annual dinner. Instead, they hired the terrific presidential biographer Ron Chernow to speak. The change made it evident to me that even in his absence, Trump can't take a joke or handle the truth. He went so far as to order his staff to boycott the event. Apparently, orange skin is very thin.

Chernow happened to be very funny that night, and in his acutely uplifting, intelligent, and humorous way, he defended the free press and the First Amendment while still getting in some hilarious shots at the president. One of my favorite lines was, "I applaud any president who aspires to the Nobel Prize for Peace. But we don't want one in the running for the Nobel Prize for Fiction." Chernow ended his sublime performance like this:

Since I've cruelly deprived you of a comedian tonight, I'd like to end with some pertinent quotes from Mark Twain, who cast a satirical eye on Washington folly. He said, "The political and commercial morals of the United States are not merely food for laughter, they are an entire banquet." And I love this quote: "Sometimes I wonder whether the world is being run by smart people who are putting us on, or by imbeciles who really mean it." He could be scathing about Capitol Hill, saying, "There is no distinctly native American criminal class except Congress." He could be equally savage about presidents, saying the US was never content "to have a chief magistrate of gold when it could get one of tin." And as we head into another election season, I will leave you with one final gem from Twain: "Politicians and diapers must be changed often, and for the same reason."

Author and CBS News journalist Eric Sevareid once said, "Next to power without honor, the most dangerous thing in the world is power without humor." And so here are some more awesome quotes from some awesome comedians about complex social issues.

BILL HICKS

I guess what surprised me the most was the discrepancy in casualties: Iraq, 150,000 casualties, USA . . . 79! Let's go over those numbers again, they're a little baffling at first. Iraq, 150,000, USA, 79. Does that mean we could have won with only eighty guys there? Just one guy in a ticker-tape parade, "I did it! Hey!"

JON STEWART

They always throw around this term: "the liberal elite." And I keep thinking to myself about the Christian right. What's more elite than believing that only you will go to heaven?

SAMANTHA BEE

Shouldn't Ted Cruz have been forced to carry his unviable campaign to term?

MICHELLE WOLF

I know a lot of you are very anti-abortion, you know, unless it's the one you got for your secret mistress. It's fun how values can waver, but good for you.

ANTHONY JESELNIK

You'll get my assault weapon when you pry it out of my curious six-year-old's cold, dead hands.

SARAH SILVERMAN

I always think I should get on it if I want to have kids. Because once you hit thirty, it can be difficult to conceive—it can be dangerous. The best time to conceive is when you're a black teenager.

DOUG STANHOPE

You never hear in the news: "Two hundred killed today when Atheist rebels took heavy shelling from the Agnostic stronghold in the North."

DAVID LETTERMAN

They say there are about 12 million illegal immigrants in this country. But if you ask a Native American, that number is more like 300 million.

CECILY STRONG

Since I'm only a comedian, I'm not going to try and tell you politicians how to do politics. That would be like you guys telling me what to do with my body. I mean, can you even imagine? Crazy.

TED ALEXANDRO

Some people say that homosexuality is a sin. It's not. God is perfectly cool with it. God feels the exact same way about homosexuality that God feels about heterosexuality. Now, you might say, "Whoa, slow down. How could you have the audacity, the temerity to speak on behalf of God?" . . . Exactly. That's an excellent point and I pray that you remember it.

ME

It seems like my kids' generation wants to get rid of gender altogether. But if we do that, how are we going to know who to pay the higher salary to?

9

Duh!
What Did You Expect?

I must say I find television very
educational. The minute somebody
turns it on, I go into the library
and read a good book.

—GROUCHO MARX

At the 2011 Iowa State Fair, presidential candidate Mitt Romney was touting his novel idea of raising taxes on people in order to keep any promises he made in regard to Social Security, Medicaid, and Medicare. A group of protesters heckled him, screaming, "Corporations!" Romney famously responded, "Corporations are people, my friend." Is that so, Mitt? Then they are the greediest, phoniest, most controlling, most humorless people in the entire world. In fact, "my friend," they are people I'd love to trip on the sidewalk or punch in the fucking face.

People assume that comedians who've appeared on television are wealthy. That couldn't be further from the truth. As I mentioned earlier, unless we go on the road or perform at corporate conferences or industry galas, we make tens of dollars for our sets in our local comedy clubs. People are shocked when I tell them that, but we have no choice. The only way for comics to be good enough to make the big bucks at high-paying corporate gigs is to perfect our acts in our home clubs. And believe me, they do feel like home. These are the places where we take the most risks. It's where we hang with other comics, grab a bite, get onstage, and figure out how far we can take a bit without any repercussions. It's our safe space. When we're hired to work for a corporation with a "brand" to uphold, or we're employed by a network, or we're representing a specific product, that's when our freedom of speech takes a nosedive. Once we accept the job, our speech is subject to the rules set by the larger entity employing us. It's our personal decision to abide by those rules or suffer the consequences of being true to ourselves.

Comedians have always faced pushback, and many comics will not, under any circumstances, censor themselves. Our personal integrity means more than a wad of cash. When we're onstage and in the zone, we never know what the fuck is going to come out of our mouths. Years ago, I was booked to do a medium-paying corporate gig at Carolines on Broadway. (I've been working at Carolines since the 1980s, when it was a small club in the Chelsea neighborhood of New York City. I've known Louis Faranda, the artistic director, since I was nineteen years old.) When I arrived at the club that night, I was handed a list of rules regarding my stand-up. These corporate people were telling me how to behave in my own home! Plus, they weren't paying me THAT much money. I happen to suffer from a mild case of ODD (oppositional defiant disorder), the clinical name for "You're not the boss of me, asshole."

When I got onstage, the first thing I did was pull out the list and read each rule aloud to the audience. One rule said I was not allowed to talk to anyone in the audience directly. Naturally, the second thing I did was to ask a guy in the front row his name. And without giving him time to respond, I said, "Oh my God! I'm so sorry! Please forgive me!" This went on the entire time I was onstage. I broke every single rule, immediately acted mortified, then profusely apologized. At the end of my set, I said, "What's with all the rules? Are you guys a cult?" The audience loved it. The head of the corporation didn't; he wanted me to apologize.

Though there was no denying I'd killed, he didn't want to pay me, but the club stuck up for me. That's another wonderful thing about a comedian's home club—they always have your back.

On October 30, 1973, John H. Douglas, an executive at CBS and an active member of Morality in Media, was driving home from a college visit to Yale with his fifteen-year-old son. He turned on WBAI, a commercial-free, listener-supported progressive radio station out of NYC. That afternoon, Paul Gorman was hosting the regularly scheduled show *Lunchpail* from 1:30 to 2:30 P.M. The topic and subsequent discussion on that particular day was societal attitudes about language. Anticipating that listeners might deem some of the material offensive, Gorman read a disclaimer, giving the audience enough time to change the station or shut off the radio. Toward the end of the program, Gorman played George Carlin's "Seven Dirty Words" routine. This didn't sit well with John H. Douglas. He couldn't believe that his angelic son had been exposed to those obscene words—and at two o'clock in the afternoon, no less! Clearly, Douglas was correct to assume that the majority of fifteen-year-old boys had never heard those words before. Give me a fucking break!

Instead of letting it go, Douglas wrote a letter to the FCC detailing the harrowing experience and included a list of the profanities he and his son had been subjected to. Douglas was incensed that any child turning the dial could be in danger of hearing such inappropriate language. He lambasted WBAI for ignoring its responsibility to the public, suggesting that the station's license be revoked. In addition to the FCC, copies of the letter were sent to public officials demanding to know how they planned to respond to such an outrage.

The thing that gets me about Douglas's tantrum is that the letter was dated December 3, 1973. He waited over a month! Imagine how hard that was for him. What with charley horses in his throat and colon from keeping his anger inside for so long, he must have been miserable to be around.

THE ABSOLUTE BEST THING about part of Mr. Douglas's grievance? It was the only letter the FCC received about the broadcast. The only one! Nobody else wrote or called to complain. Apparently, everyone else in the tristate area was too busy with their early Christmas shopping. But Mr. Douglas was determined that this should never happen again—especially to innocent teenagers. Mr. Douglas was concerned about how those words would turn his son and other impressionable children into immoral people. I can see his point. Charles Manson, Ted Bundy, Jeffrey Dahmer—each could pinpoint his irrepressible urge to butcher people to the moment they first heard someone utter the word *cunt*.

The FCC started an investigation and eventually issued a declaratory order granting the complaint but not imposing any formal sanctions. So, there was a bit of a reprimand, but no fine. The FCC also said that if it received any more complaints, it would take them into consideration when Pacifica, which owned WBAI, renewed its radio license. Two of the FCC commissioners did not agree with the decision. After another petition was filed, the FCC said that it "never intended to place an absolute prohibition on the broadcast of this type of language, but rather sought to channel it to times of day when children would least likely be exposed to it." So, children should not be exposed to such filthy language coming from the radio during the morning hours; they should only be able to hear those words on the playground, in the car when some asshole in the other lane cuts off their mother, or at the dinner table when their abusive alcoholic father doesn't like the meal his wife has placed in front of him.

After the second decision was issued, a Petition for Clarification or Reconsideration was filed with the FCC. Then came yet another opinion, then it was to the Court of Appeals for the D.C. Circuit, then the D.C. Circuit Court reversed the order, and in 1978 it finally ended up in the Supreme Court of the United States, *Federal Communications Commission v. Pacifica Foundation,* where the First Amendment lost. The FCC won the case in a 5–4 decision that made it clear that the government does have the power to restrict certain broadcasts on the basis of language. Wait, what? Don't the conservatives want *less* government intervention into our private lives? The Notorious RBG (Justice Ruth Bader Ginsburg) has stated that she disagreed with this decision, but it has held its place in restricting language and invoking censorship on radio and television. I should also mention that Morality in Media is still going strong. It's now called the National Center on Sexual Exploitation, and it really confronts this pressing issue. Among its "Dirty Dozen," a list of the twelve leading "facilitators of sexual exploitation," are such offenders as HBO, Amazon, the *Sports Illustrated* Swimsuit Issue, Roku, Google, and Twitter. They also want to ban *Cosmopolitan* magazine from supermarkets because of the way it exploits women. There's a donate button on their website, if you're so inclined.

When I think of the FCC's standards, one name always comes to mind—Howard Stern. Between 1990 and 2004, the FCC issued Howard fines totaling two and a half million dollars. Two and a half million dollars! A shock jock is making the world a dangerous place. Give me a big fat hairy break. At least we can trust the US Treasury to put the money to good use, like it always does.

Now, nobody can push the envelope like Howard. His humor is brazen, unabashed, and sometimes even shocking—hence the title "shock jock." Howard is one person in show business who's never, ever compromised his true self for anyone or anything. And believe me, he's been tested from day one.

I've been a fan of Howard's since 1982, when I started listening to him on WNBC radio. I also must say that *The Howard Stern Show*, which ran on WWOR-TV from July 1990 until August 1992, was the highlight of my week for those two years.

There are many sources you can peruse to learn about Howard's radio career (the most recent being his bestselling book *Howard Stern Comes Again*), how he got his start, the challenges he's faced along the way, and how 99 percent of morning radio show hosts around the country are all copycats of Howard, Robin Quivers, and the gang. For now, I'm going to focus solely on his battles with censorship.

In 1982, Howard had been working at WWDC in Washington, D.C., when WNBC radio approached him with a job offer. He took the job at WNBC, and he was psyched to be on air in New York City, his hometown. For Howard, it was a dream come true; this was the radio he'd listened to while driving in the car with his dad. In Howard's *New York Times*–bestselling book *Private Parts,* he describes how, during their initial negotiations, WNBC had assured him that they would also bring his producer, Fred Norris, and newsreader and sidekick, Robin Quivers, to New York. During his meeting with NBC management while he was still in D.C., station executives asked Robin and Fred what they would do if they weren't hired for the new show. In *Private Parts,* Howard says he ignored the question because he was focusing on other aspects of the meeting and, presumably, it had already been decided that Fred and Robin would be joining him in New York. We later find out that it had been NBC's intention all along to bring Howard to New York alone so they would have more control over him. Later, in an article published by *New York* magazine that Howard quotes in his book, Bob Sherman, the executive vice president of WNBC at the time, admitted, "We wanted Howard without his aides-de-camp, so he'd be as naked and vulnerable as possible to good management."

This pisses me off on so many levels, but definitely nowhere near as much as it pissed off Howard. So, you want Howard and his ratings, but you want to control how he behaves and what he says? He had the ratings he had BECAUSE of the way he behaved and the things he said! Who the fuck did these people think they were? Because some of Howard's jokes and bits can be classified as juvenile, does that mean he should be treated like a child?

It gets worse.

Howard had done some interviews about being a shock jock, so when a man named Douglas Kiker, an anchor on a new TV show called *NBC Magazine*—a knockoff of CBS's *60 Minutes*—asked for an interview, Howard was all in. (It should be noted that Howard actually signed his contract with WNBC during the filming of this interview, so of course it would be favorable, because Kiker and Howard were working for the same company.) I looked EVERYWHERE for this piece, entitled "X-Rated Radio," but it seems to have been sealed in a lockbox and squirreled away in some secret cave that nobody has access to. To give you the best picture possible of the interview, I'll need to quote Howard directly from his book. Also, I don't think a guy named Kiker should ever be assigned a story that involves a Jew, but that's a discussion for another time.

Kiker opens the story with the following introduction:

What you're about to hear is going to shock you because it's vulgar, even obscene. A warning: If there are any children in the room, you might not want them to watch

this report. It's X-rated radio, barnyard radio, and there's
more and more of it on the air because kids love it.

Howard says, "Then they went to a close-up of a radio and
coming out of that radio was the voice of, you guessed it, me!! 'I
hear your pappy is so disgusting that he takes a bubble bath by
farting in a mud puddle.'"

The book goes on to describe Kiker (I laugh every single time I
type that name) telling the story of his seven-year-old son coming
down to breakfast and repeating Howard's mud puddle line word
for word. How appalling! For every comedian I know, that would
have been a funny and proud parenting story, but not for those
who are so much better than us because they speak so eloquently
and attend church every Sunday.

Remember, Howard thought it was going to be a positive report. He's there watching with his wife, all excited about the cov-
erage, and they see a hatchet job! You know what, Mr. Kiker? If I
don't mind my child being exposed to the words *fart, prostitute,
ass, penis, vagina,* etc., what business is that of yours? George
Carlin said it best when he said this about the "Seven Words You
Can Never Say on Television" (or radio):

Language can't hurt people. If these words could be
shown to truly create moral problems for people, I'd have
to take another look at it. But I don't think there is a shred
of evidence that the use of bad language in any way
makes the person a bad person.

To make matters worse, before Howard's first show on
WNBC, he was given a list of things he couldn't say on the air.
Ready?[1]

1. Slander, defamation, or personal attacks on private individuals unless they have consented or are a part of the act.
2. Jokes or sketches relating to personal tragedies.
3. Jokes dealing with sickness or death.
4. Jokes dealing with sexual topics in a lascivious manner.
5. Scatological or other "barnyard"-type material.
6. Ridiculing religion for the sake of ridicule or making fun of the religious faith people may have.
7. Use of the so-called seven dirty words.

I don't know where to begin. You hire someone because he has the best ratings, brings in lots of advertisers, and is beloved by his listeners, and then try to censor him right before he's about to go on the air for the first time??? Look, we all know this was about one thing—money. Antiseptic, untalented executives should keep their hands out of the creative. But money is power.

Nobody was going to tame Howard. And why would they even try? Howard's persona was influenced by the conservative radio host Bob Grant. Bob's show aired on WABC during drive time, and I remember listening to it in the car after school. Bob was an angry guy. He'd take calls and then insult the callers, oftentimes hanging up on them. He was rude and obnoxious. He had an attitude and a very distinctive point of view. He was defiantly himself, and Howard admired that. As Howard readily admits these days, as a young man, he, himself, was full of rage. Due to his commitment to psychotherapy and self-examination, he's evolved. Some people don't like the new Howard. Too bad for them.

One of the largest fines Howard ever received was for a joke he made on air in 1992: "The closest I came to making love to a black woman was I masturbated to a picture of Aunt Jemima on a pancake box."

Did you laugh? The FCC certainly didn't. Truthfully, I suspect they probably *did* laugh—and then fined Infinity Broadcasting Corporation, Howard's boss, $600,000. Yes. Six hundred thousand dollars! Howard didn't say any of the seven words, and yet just the idea, the visual people formed in their heads, was obscene enough for the FCC. Let's keep in mind that this was the era when every afternoon, you could turn on any of the major networks and find tabloid trash television. You didn't need to visualize anything on these shows—they showed everything. Every day, after school—when kids were supposedly doing their homework.

The Howard Stern Show is on in the morning, and Howard likes it that way. He's said that he's doing the Lord's work by making people laugh during the most miserable part of their day: their morning commute to an unfulfilling job. His ultimate goal? To entertain. In 1995, Howard was the subject of a segment by John Stossel for the ABC show *20/20*. Stossel not only interviewed Howard for this but also sat in the studio with Howard and the gang while they were on the air. He observed Howard hosting one of his signature bits, "Black Jeopardy." (In the past few years, *SNL* has had a sporadically recurring bit also called "Black Jeopardy." Hmmmmm.) Three African American men competed in the game, answering (in the form of a question, of course) clues from categories that included "Bang Bang Bang," "Dark Meat, White Meat," and "If You Scream, I'll Kill You." In the segment, Stossel seems quite judgmental and later asks Howard, "Is it funny enough? Don't you make life worse for some people?" If you're wondering why the fuck he'd ask that kind of question, it was meant to imply that Howard was encouraging racism. Racism? Those "Black Jeopardy" contestants were thrilled to be there.

How the hell was Howard making life worse for anyone? What Howard does is expose racism as well as the racist's stupidity, and for good reason. Howard grew up in a black neighborhood, where all everyone did was talk about race. He makes fun of stereotypes; he doesn't have racist feelings. And if he did, we'd know it—in the same way we'd know if he were a misogynist. Howard has been called a misogynist, a sexist, a chauvinist pig, and more, yet he's NEVER been accused of behaving inappropriately with women. You can also be certain that smart and classy Robin Quivers would not work with a racist or a misogynist.

One of my favorite things Stossel said to Howard was, "People hate you." Seriously? How is someone supposed to respond to that? What's the purpose of saying something so fucking nasty? To make Howard cry? Spare me, John. When Howard tried to engage Stossel as he was sitting in during the live radio broadcast, Stossel wouldn't bite. He didn't want to talk about anything personal—especially his wife and kids. I'll hazard a guess here that John Stossel isn't much fun to hang out with. But in his favor, Stossel sided with Howard on the government intervening in what is appropriate for children.

One of Howard's best guests ever? Donald Trump, of course! Trump lacks an edit button and would take the bait and say anything and everything—like how hot his daughter is, and how he had broached the idea of an abortion with Marla Maples when she was pregnant. Howard exposes truth, stupidity, and hypocrisy, and welcomes tension with open arms. He's well aware, as we all are, that what people say in private is much different from what they say in public. Howard's guests are there voluntarily. They know exactly what he's about.

Howard endured a lot of crap from the FCC, especially follow-ing his 1987 anti-FCC rally in New York City, which was attended by two thousand people. In 2006, Howard moved to SiriusXM radio with the slogan "Join the Revolution." He has no restric-tions on SiriusXM and has since become one of the most compel-ling interviewers of our generation. He's apologized to and made amends with celebrities he used to diss on a regular basis, such as Kathie Lee Gifford, Rosie O'Donnell, and David Letterman. He attributes much of his success to "always being honest with the audience," even when he's angry. We could use a bit of honesty in this country right now.

Full disclosure: Years ago, Don Buchwald & Associates, the agency that represents Howard, also represented me. During that time, I went in and pitched a TV show to Howard at his studio offices. He was a mensch. I've pitched a lot of shows to producers in my career, but pitching to Howard was different. He was warm and open—and he really listened. A few days later, I was in my apartment and my phone rang. The voice on the other end said, "Hi, it's Howard." I said, "Howard??" I thought it was my good friend Howard from college, but this voice was way deeper. Then he said, "Stern." I almost shit in my pants. *Howard Stern is calling me at home?* He asked me how I was, and then said, "I wanted to call you personally, and I say this with a heavy heart, but we are not going to be able to produce your show at this time. We have so many projects in the fire, and it's just not the right time for us." He went on to compliment me and wish me good luck with my fu-ture endeavors. I can tell you right now that in my over thirty-five years in this business, nobody has EVER taken time out of their day—or had the courtesy and respect to call me personally—to tell me the truth. During the call, Howard was kind, caring, and decent enough to treat me like a human being. I've bumped into

Howard a few times since, and he's been nothing but a true gentleman. He's a class act.

If you're a fan of comedy, and even if you're not, I'm pretty sure you've heard of the Friars Club. It's a fraternal organization made up of comedians, celebrities, their representatives, and various wealthy people willing to pay dues to sit near a funny person at lunch. The Friars Club is mostly known for its annual roasts, where the guest of honor is celebrated by a dais of comedians and other notables who each take their turn at a podium to make as much fun of the honoree as possible. The Friars's motto is, "We only roast the ones we love!" It's true. The roasts originated as a no-holds-barred closed-door event where everyone would let loose. The audience gets to witness how comics show their love: by mocking the hell out of each other. The first televised roast aired in 1968, followed by one annually for the next three years. The first *Dean Martin Celebrity Roast* aired in 1974, and multiple roasts followed until 1984. In 1998, Comedy Central, in conjunction with the Friars Club, produced and televised its first roast, and after four years, the channel decided to produce the roasts on its own. Many other networks have also produced their own roasts. Why not? They're filled with celebrities, they're usually very funny, and they tend to get good ratings. But there's also a downside to their ubiquity, because unlike the original closed-door roasts, many of the roasters who appear on TV don't know the roastee personally.

There have been a lot of controversies surrounding the roasts over the years, like in 1993, when Ted Danson showed up in blackface and used racist epithets while roasting his then girlfriend, Whoopi Goldberg. (They really should leave the actual roasting to the comedians, but money talks.) Another notorious incident occurred at the Friars Club roast of *Playboy* magazine founder Hugh

Hefner, which was held only three weeks after 9/11. During his turn at the podium, the hilarious Gilbert Gottfried joked, "I have to catch a flight to California. I can't get a direct flight. They said they have to stop at the Empire State Building first." A few people laughed but most gasped and booed and the words "too soon" were heard loud and clear. Having completely lost the crowd, and figuring he had no place to go but further down, Gilbert told the "Aristocrats" joke (more on this in a minute). Amazingly, he won the audience back and left them cheering. Both the 9/11 and "Aristocrats" jokes were scrubbed out when Comedy Central aired the roast that November—sparing Gilbert a lot of grief. That was pretty much the end of the incident (except that the story of that night has become legendary—at least among other comedians), and Gilbert and everyone else went back to their lives. It was lucky for him that Comedy Central made the decision to leave those jokes on the cutting room floor. Other times, Gilbert wouldn't be so fortunate.

"The Aristocrats" is a legendary improvised joke. It begins and ends the same way each time it's told. The setup is that a family walks into a talent agent's office to pitch him their act. The joke teller improvises a detailed description of the act, which consists of the filthiest, most disgusting, vulgar, scatological, tasteless, and repulsive things you've ever heard of. The agent, shocked (or possibly intrigued), inquires about the name of the act and is told, "The Aristocrats!!" There's a 2005 documentary about the joke, appropriately titled *The Aristocrats*. It's not for the faint of heart, but it's hilarious. I appear in it, nine months pregnant, saying the most vile and odious things I could think of. My mother was thrilled.

Comedians love to push the envelope because it feels so rewarding to lead people into a state of discomfort and then release

them from it with a smart and unexpected punch line. Without
freedom of speech, we couldn't do that. Though the First Amendment was designed to prevent the US government from impinging
on its citizens' ability to speak freely, it doesn't prohibit employ-
ers from shutting up their employees. Ira Glasser told me that:

> When the country was first started, the understanding
> when they passed the First Amendment, the understanding
> that most people had of what constituted free speech
> and what the First Amendment protected, was that it
> protected true speech, but it didn't protect lying, it didn't
> protect false speech.

He went on to say, "And so what happened over time—and it
didn't happen right away—is that the founders themselves began
to understand that if you wanted to protect true speech, you have
to be willing to protect false speech, or at least speech that was
accused of being false."

In our country, freedom of speech means freedom of ALL
speech, even if it's critical of the government. Unfortunately,
when it comes to speaking truth to power on national television,
the brave in the vanguard are often among the first casualties.

When discussing the topic of censorship on television, the
one show that always comes up, and rightly so, is *The Smothers
Brothers Comedy Hour*. I remember watching the show in my family's den on our black-and-white Zenith TV when I was a little
girl. I was way too young to understand it fully, but it was en-
tertaining because Tommy and Dick Smothers were very funny
together. This was the 1960s, when watching TV was a family
activity. One of the great things about the show was that its guests
appealed to viewers of all ages. For older viewers, they would

have more button-down musical guests like Mel Tormé, Harry Belafonte, and Kate Smith perform on the same show with bands and performers such as The Who, Joan Baez, Pete Seeger, and The Doors, who attracted younger viewers.

The show also had some of the best young writers of the time, writers like Rob Reiner, Steve Martin, Mason Williams, and Bob Einstein. The Smothers brothers preferred younger writers because at that time, millions of young people were not happy with the war in Vietnam, segregation, President Lyndon B. Johnson's policies, and so much more. It was a radical time for young liberals; they were very pissed off, and for good reason. (Younger people today are so PC that they'd probably object to some of the skits and songs that appeared on the show over fifty years ago.) Remember when young people were fighting for freedom of speech and expression? Those were the days, my friend.

David Bianculli wrote a great book called *Dangerously Funny: The Uncensored Story of "The Smothers Brothers Comedy Hour."* I give you permission to read it—after you finish my book. I listened to a 2009 interview Bianculli did on NPR's *Fresh Air,* and yes, I know I just said NPR, so calm down. After listening to the interview and doing some more research, I was dumbfounded at the number of network television shows from the 1960s and '70s that would never see the light of day today. One thing Bianculli said that resonated with me was that while Elvis Presley was able to resume his career after leaving show business for two years to serve in the US Army, and Muhammad Ali bounced back after he was stripped of his boxing titles for refusing military service, once Tommy and Dick Smothers lost their TV platform, they never had a comeback. Is it me, or do comedians' and satirists' misdeeds keep them persona non grata for inordinately longer periods than those of other celebrity offenders?

What was especially egregious about the ending of *The Smothers Brothers Comedy Hour* was that the show wasn't canceled—in fact, it had already been renewed for another season. What really happened was that Tommy and Dick Smothers were abruptly fired. Everything was perfectly fine for the first nine episodes. Then the comedic genius Elaine May wrote a skit in which she and Tommy played movie censors watching questionable clips. They portrayed the censors as really getting off on editing stuff out of the films. Apparently, it was hilarious. (How could it not be, if Elaine May wrote it?) Unfortunately, nobody, except for the studio audience, got to see it, because it never aired. The network censors censored the censor skit! So-called moral experts have NO sense of humor. It's wonderful that they're still deciding what's funny.

The Smothers brothers made fun of President Johnson a lot, and yet Johnson's daughters, Lynda and Luci, were vocal fans of the show. LBJ was so incensed by one episode that he called William Paley, then head of CBS, at home at three o'clock in the morning to complain about how he was being depicted. The president seemed especially annoyed that the cast was so vocal in their distaste for the Vietnam War while there were US soldiers still over there fighting. Tommy agreed to lay off, but only if they'd allow Pete Seeger to sing a few songs on the show. In the early 1950s, Seeger had been banned from appearing on commercial TV because of his politics; by this time, 1967, the ban had stretched for almost seventeen years. CBS acquiesced, and Seeger was booked on the show—where he proceeded to sing an anti-war song. CBS was not pleased.

The censors at CBS really made life miserable for the show. Bill Tankersley was the network's head of censorship, and he had a lot of power. Also, the set of standards broadcasters were using at the time, known as "The Code of Practices," didn't seem strict enough for CBS.

It got to the point where the network had to okay the script on Wednesday in advance of the Friday taping before a live audience. To put this into perspective, think about this: *SNL* does a rehearsal show in front of a live audience at eight P.M. on Saturday night, less than four hours before the show airs. Some people prefer to attend the rehearsal because they'll get to see all the bits that get cut from the actual broadcast. Decisions about which material makes it on air are being made right up until showtime. Being required to hand in a script two days before shooting for a show that thrives on social commentary is absolutely ridiculous. A lot can happen in forty-eight hours, as we can all attest to these days.

It didn't stop there. Some CBS affiliates also wanted to pre-screen episodes, since their local audiences were more conservative leaning and they didn't want to piss off their viewers ($$$$$$). Just imagine groups of Mike Pences and Jerry Falwells deciding which satire and comedy is appropriate for us to watch.

Tangent Time!

What exactly do these religious zealots find funny? What do they laugh at? Knock-knock jokes? How the Lord created the earth in six days, but it takes me longer to do my laundry? My friend the VERY funny comedian Ted Alexandro has THE BEST Jesus joke:

Have you ever been in church, preacher's preaching, choir's singing, you look up at the crucifix and think, "Wow . . . Jesus had great abs"? Because he was cut, could have had his own workout videos, like *Abs of a Savior, Body of Christ, Cross Training.* Because that's what you want in a savior. You want him to be in shape. Because have you seen Buddha? Sloppy! Sloppy, sloppy, slopp-ola. A few crunches, Budd! Clean it up. The last supper shouldn't last forever.

This joke doesn't disparage any religious beliefs whatsoever. It's observational—and hilarious! Recently, Ted posted on social media about how a "Christian" had confronted him about that bit. Here's the story in his own words:

I had an elderly woman at a casino come up to me and say, "I didn't care for your jokes about Jesus." I said, "Oh, I'm sorry you feel that way." She said, "I found it offensive that you would make jokes about my Lord and Savior. It wasn't funny." I said, "My apologies. Have fun gambling."

Touché, Ted!

Okay, back to the Smothers brothers. I feel terrible when I think about how hard Tommy Smothers fought for his freedom of speech. One of the most proactive things he did was to regularly give the press a heads-up about what was happening at the show. The newspapers helped to get the real behind-the-scenes story out. Tommy did everything he could to keep the public informed, but he still got screwed in the end. The show was groundbreaking and set the stage for *SNL, The Daily Show,* Bill Maher's *Politically Incorrect* and *Real Time, The Colbert Report, Full Frontal with Samantha Bee, Last Week Tonight with John Oliver,* and many, many others. *The Smothers Brothers Comedy Hour* achieved the impossible. It was the first successful show to air during what was considered the worst time slot, Sunday night at nine P.M., opposite NBC's huge hit show *Bonanza*. At the time, television was the one big escape from real-life stresses. There were only a few networks, and most entertainment shows were fictional sitcoms. *The Smothers Brothers Comedy Hour* wasn't pretend, and it dealt with a counterculture that many people preferred to forget about while they were home relaxing.

The show ran for only three seasons, yet despite its short run and the obstacles thrown in its path, it accomplished a lot. Comedian Pat Paulsen announced his first campaign for president on the show, and comic David Steinberg delivered sermonettes mocking some of the ridiculousness of religion. (And he should know a lot about that, since he's the son of a strict rabbi and studied theology in Israel.) The skits did not please the powers that be, however, and Steinberg's first sermonette was cut from an early episode. In the third season, Tommy encouraged Steinberg to do an impromptu sermonette. That was the last straw for CBS. The show was terminated.

The censors were supposedly there to protect the American public, yet who the fuck are they to decide what I need protection from? Tankersley was responsible for putting Rob and Laura Petrie into single beds on *The Dick Van Dyke Show*. He also rejected a laxative commercial that was scheduled to run during the *CBS Evening News*. Can you imagine? You cannot turn on network TV today without seeing commercials for erectile dysfunction, vaginal dryness, Peyronie's disease, periods, adult diapers, and a bunch of other things I don't need to hear about while I'm watching March Madness with my kids. (To be fair, vaginal dryness and tampon commercials are rarely aired during sporting events because everyone knows that only cis males appreciate sports.)

After the show was taken off the air, Tommy Smothers apologized to LBJ for giving him such a hard time. President Johnson wrote back to him and said, "It is part of the price of leadership of this great and free nation to be the target of clever satirists. You have given the gift of laughter to our people. May we never grow so somber or self-important that we fail to appreciate the humor in our lives." Wow. Can you imagine for one second that Donald Trump could or would EVER write something even remotely like that to *SNL*?

In 1968, the show ended up being nominated for an Emmy award, and the writers and producers all attended the Emmys thinking that *Laugh-In* would win again. But when one of the presenters, Paul Lynde, read out the names of *The Smothers Brothers*'s writers, the cameras cut to Tommy Smothers sitting there with a big smile on his face. Though he was the head writer, he didn't go up onstage to accept the award because he'd withdrawn his name due to the negativity and controversy associated with him.

In 1973, Dick and Tommy sued CBS. Though the brothers won the case and were awarded damages, the sum was far less than the amount they'd sued for. I wish I could've been a fly on the wall while the CBS attorneys were reading some of the "offensive" bits that had aired on the show. THAT must have been funny.

At the 2008 Emmy Awards, Steve Martin presented Tommy Smothers with the 1968 Emmy that he had so deserved forty years prior. Tommy's acceptance speech was perfect. "Freedom of speech and freedom of expression aren't really important . . . unless they're heard. So, the freedom of hearing is just as important as the freedom of speaking." He went on to say, "There is nothing more scary than watching ignorance in action." He dedicated the Emmy to "all people who feel compelled to speak out and not afraid to speak to power. And won't shut up. And refuse to be silenced."

Thank you, Tommy.

After the disappointment of *The Smothers Brothers Comedy Hour,* the tide of change in our country intensified. The sexual revolution, along with the civil rights, gay rights, and women's liberation movements, drastically expanded what people thought of as acceptable. Comedy had a big hand in the process. Comedians and society worked in tandem, with society giving comedians permission to tackle previously off-limit topics, and comedians, in turn, using humor to make discussing those topics less threatening.

Beginning in the early 1970s, when huge numbers of Americans were watching the same television shows at the same exact times, television writers and producers Norman Lear and James L. Brooks literally created the zeitgeist. At work or school, what did people talk about? The previous night's episodes of the decade's groundbreaking television shows—*All in The Family, Maude, The Jeffersons, The Mary Tyler Moore Show, One Day at a Time, M*A*S*H, Good Times, Sanford and Son.* Besides having unforgettable theme songs (the *Mary Tyler Moore Show* theme is my ringtone), these multicamera sitcoms wrestled with topics that the Smothers brothers could never approach. How did they get away with it? Lear, Brooks, and a few others created characters that mirrored the good, the bad, and the ugly in all of us. We grew attached to Archie and Edith, George and Weezy, Maude, Hawkeye, Radar, and the rest. They became part of our own families, and whatever issues they were dealing with fostered dialogues in our family rooms, offices, schools, and places of worship. When they got blindsided or suffered a setback, we empathized. When one of them passed away, we mourned.

When NBC decided to stop airing reruns of *The Tonight Show Starring Johnny Carson* at eleven thirty on Saturday nights, they took a chance on a new variety show. *Saturday Night Live* went on the air on October 11, 1975, building on what the Smothers brothers had created and bringing it to another level. The inaugural host was George Carlin, the musical guests were Billy Preston and Janis Ian. The writers and the cast of the "Not Ready for Prime Time Players" threw themselves headfirst into the political sphere, mocking presidents and other powerful officials, parodying our culture, and taking risks like we'd never seen before on TV. Over four decades later, the show still continues to ruffle feathers and satirize what is otherwise sacrosanct. As it was after the terrorist attacks of 9/11, it remains the arbiter of when it's appropriate to laugh. Mayor Rudy Giuliani, surrounded by shell-shocked first responders, opened the first episode of SNL following the tragedy by saying "Our hearts are broken, but they are beating; and they are beating stronger than ever." After Paul Simon sang "The Boxer," Lorne Michaels joined New York City's heroes onstage, and the mayor told him that "SNL is one of New York City's greatest institutions and that's why it's important for you to do your show." Michaels looked at the mayor and asked, "Can we be funny?" To which Giuliani responded, "Why start now?"

It was at that exact moment that our nation was not only given permission to laugh, but permission to heal. Sadly, it's clear from Giuliani's recent behavior that the former mayor no longer holds SNL's comedy and its role in American culture in high regard. It's pathetic to see him sacrificing his heart, soul, and whatever rudimentary funny bone he had defending the fascist gaseous windbag who at the time I'm writing this is currently defiling the White House.

We can't deny the power of TV to increase the visibility of minorities. Over the past five decades, things have progressed quite a bit, and we can now turn on our televisions and see more accurate and complex portrayals of African Americans, Asians, Latinos, people with disabilities, LGBTQ people, Jews, immigrants, and every other minority, though there's still work to be done—especially on network television. The list of acceptable topics for late-night hosts and stand-up comedians has grown substantially, yet in many ways, we've gone backward. Why? Two words: *political correctness*. To be more precise: the proselytization of political correctness by the sanctimonious left. Yes, you heard me.

When *All in The Family* debuted in 1971, CBS issued a warning for the first six episodes. In 2019, when ABC aired live re-creations of *All in the Family* and *The Jeffersons* using the original scripts and starring some of the biggest names in TV today, the shows were edited. The network played a long bleep over George Jefferson's utterance of the N-word. During the original airing, the word wasn't bleeped, and throughout both shows' original runs, neither were the words *fag, spic, chink,* and *kike*. They are horrible words, but there was no denying that they were brazenly spoken by many Americans who were just like Archie Bunker. In some ways, these shows were truly the first reality television.

In season one of Norman Lear's hit show *Maude,* a spin-off of *All in the Family,* there was a two-part episode called "Maude's Dilemma." The title character, Maude Findlay, a forty-seven-year-old women's libber, married to her fourth husband, Walter, finds herself pregnant. Already a mother (and grandmother), she's faced with the decision of whether to keep the baby. The previous year on *All in the Family,* Sally Struthers's character, Gloria Stivic, had suffered a miscarriage, so Lear wanted to steer away from repeating that scenario. After processing all her emotions and taking into account those of her feminist daughter, Carol, Maude decides to have an abortion. (The word *abortion* was mentioned only once in each half of the two-part episode.)

The episode confronted families with the realities of unwanted pregnancy and women's rights. Though "Maude's Dilemma" hasn't aired on network TV in the twenty-first century so far, Walter's last words to Maude after she asks him if she's doing the right thing should be the current motto for the pro-choice movement: "For you, Maude, for me, in the privacy of our own lives, you're doing the right thing." CBS did the right thing by airing the episode, though it should be duly noted that the decision was made after Lear threatened to take the hit show (a huge moneymaker for the network) off the air for good.

Money may talk, but it definitely doesn't have a sense of humor. Gilbert Gottfried was gainfully employed as the voice of the insurance giant Aflac's duck mascot. After the deadly 2011 tsunami in Japan, Gilbert's fans tweeted at him asking for some jokes. Because he has the neural pathways of a comedian, Gilbert did what comedians do after a tragedy and obliged. Granted, this was when Twitter didn't have the power to elect the leader of the free world. Here are a few of Gilbert's gems:

> I just split up with my girlfriend, but like the Japanese say, "They'll be another one floating by any minute now."
>
> ——
>
> I was talking to my Japanese real estate agent. I said, "Is there a school in this area?" She said, "Not now, but just wait."
>
> ——
>
> What does every Japanese person have in their apartment? Flood lights.

Hilarious, right? Obviously not to Aflac, which does 75 percent of its business in Japan. Oops! Gilbert was fired immediately. Aflac's certainly entitled to pick and choose their spokespeople, but perhaps one of the corporate executives could have checked out Gilbert's sense of humor before giving him a contract. After his firing, Gilbert issued this statement: "I sincerely apologize to anyone who was offended by my attempt at humor regarding the tragedy in Japan. I meant no disrespect, and my thoughts are with the victims and their families."

If you're thinking, *There is no way Gilbert Gottfried wrote that,* you're absolutely correct. It was something his representatives forced him to do, and he resents it to this day. Gilbert described the incident to me this way: "You wake up every day and eat a bowl of cornflakes, and then one day you wake up, eat a bowl of cornflakes, and all hell breaks loose." That's exactly right. You're a comedian known for making inappropriate jokes who, one day, does exactly what you've always done, and suddenly you're the biggest miscreant in the world. He's used to it.

At the 1991 Emmy Awards, Gilbert presented the Emmy for Outstanding Writing in a Variety or Music Program. This was right after Paul Reubens was arrested for masturbating in an adult theater in Sarasota, Florida. Since the arrest was fresh in people's minds, Gilbert addressed it, once again doing his job as a comedian. He walked out onstage, telling the orchestra to shut up. Then, at the podium, he said:

> I want to get something off my chest. You know, I'll tell you something, ladies and gentlemen, I sleep a lot better since Pee-wee Herman's been arrested. If masturbation is a crime, I should be on death row! If masturbation is against the law, I should have been sent to the electric chair years ago! To think that by age fourteen I was already Al Capone. Right now, I'm like Superman. You can put charcoal in my hands, and I can crush it into a diamond. It's like if the police tried

to arrest me, it'd be, "Quick! Stay away from his right hand!"
Your puny weapons can't hurt me!

The audience applauded, and Gilbert said, "Please, only clap if you like masturbation. Now on to our category that can be described in a way that women have never described me—long and hard." He then read the nominees, the winners accepted their award, and that was that.

When Gilbert got offstage, no one really paid any attention to him because there were so many other big celebrities there to fawn over. Afterward, at an Emmy party, someone told him that his masturbation jokes weren't going to air on the Los Angeles feed in a couple of hours. He was informed that the producers were livid, and that one of them said that if he ran into Gilbert, he would kick his ass. So mature. If you watch the video, you'll hear how much the audience is eating up Gilbert's jokes. They loved his material so much that there were applause breaks as well. But when the press got ahold of the story, they presented it as if everyone in the room had been shocked and offended. Come on!

A few months after all this bullshit, something curious happened that pissed Gilbert off. "What gets me is like a few months later, *Seinfeld* does an episode on masturbation, and it's *Citizen Kane*." Bingo! An epic episode of *Seinfeld* about masturbation called "The Contest" aired on network TV in prime time and elicited nothing but accolades. And guess which show won the Emmy award for Outstanding Writing in a Comedy Series that year? You got it! Gilbert wasn't there to give the *Seinfeld* team their award. In fact, he's never been invited back to appear on the Emmys.

For a comedian, all of this is exceptionally frustrating, but the executives at Fox were completely within their rights to not air the masturbation jokes. Gilbert was their employee, and the material he wrote was work for hire. If I had an office job (which I wouldn't, or rather, couldn't—I'd throw myself down an elevator shaft after five minutes in a cubicle) and interrupted an executive who was in the middle of giving a presentation by saying, "Oh my God, you're so fucking uptight! Can someone please blow this guy?" I'd get fired.

Unquestionably, it was NBC's right to air "The Contest." *Seinfeld* was a huge hit, and the comedy business, like every other business in the United States, is all about the money. Every day at their jobs, people make decisions they'd never make at home simply because they have a family to feed. But when it comes to employing a comedian, it's the comedian's personal decision to abide by the rules or suffer the consequences of being true to who they are.

10

Can We Talk? Please?

I'd much rather be a woman than a
man. Women can cry, they can wear
cute clothes, and they're the first to be
rescued off sinking ships.

—GILDA RADNER

Just in case I forgot to mention it, I happen to be a Jew. I grew up in a kosher home, had a bat mitzvah, was forced to attend Hebrew high school, and didn't try lobster until I was in my twenties (though I took my first bong hit at sixteen). If you assume that the Jewish commandments regarding food, keeping the sabbath, and being constipated for eight days from eating matzoh are the most difficult to adhere to, you're wrong. The laws that are the hardest (i.e., virtually impossible) to keep are the ones regarding speech—improper speech. Jewish laws regarding the tongue are some of the basic tenets of the religion. The reason? Once something's said, you can't take it back.

Gossip, slander, and words used to intentionally embarrass someone are MAJOR sins, on par with idolatry, adultery, and murder. The Talmud says, "He who publicly shames his neighbor is as though he shed blood." The most surprising aspect of these laws? The listener is considered even more of a sinner than the gossiper. Why? Because gossip only exists if someone else hears it. The Eighth Commandment states, "Thou shalt not bear false witness against thy neighbor," which includes false flattery. Wait, what? Are you kidding me? How the hell did so many Jews get into show business, then? "You look fabulous!! Your audition was perfect!! Did you lose weight? Is it me, or do you just keep getting younger? Whatever you're doing . . . it's working."

One of the great things about Judaism is that it fosters free thinking. Talmudic scholars have been arguing over the same texts for more than two thousand years, trying to divine what God really meant about this and that. What makes a bar or bat mitzvah (FYI, they now have b-mitzvahs for those who are gender fluid—"Today I am a them!") such a momentous occasion in a Jewish child's life is not that it marks the point when he, she, or they truly become an adult; it's that their opinion, their voice, is now taken seriously. Just think about what happens at a bat mitzvah—the girl reads aloud a passage from the Torah that corresponds to her birthday, then gives a speech (d'var Torah) about her interpretation of that particular passage and how it is relevant to her current life. There's no right or wrong here. As Jews, we're encouraged to think outside the box and interpret things personally. (Good for me, since I take everything personally.)

Whenever people ask me why there are so many Jewish comedians, I explain that we're taught to look at situations from all possible perspectives. I also point out that this is probably why there are so many Jewish lawyers, and why enjoying something can't just be the end of it.

This brings me to the reason why so many Jewish women have immersed themselves in the seemingly endless struggle for human rights, using words, speech, and freedom of expression to change the world. Do yourself a favor and learn about some of these women: Sarah Schenirer, Emma Goldman, Emma Lazarus, Ray Frank, Justine Wise Polier, Anna Sokolow, Hannah Greenebaum Solomon, Henrietta Szold, Lillian Wald, Gertrude Weil, Anne Frank, Bella Abzug, Betty Friedan, Letty Cottin Pogrebin,

Golda Meir, Nadine Gordimer, Gloria Steinem (her father was Jewish, so we're claiming her), Carole King, Judy Blume, Ruth Bader Ginsburg, Roberta Kaplan . . . I know there are so many more names I should include here, but I have a deadline. And please forgive me for putting together such a long list, but I feel compelled to make up for the hit the Jewish brand has recently taken by having such awful representatives as Jeffrey Epstein, Stephen Miller, Jared Kushner, Harvey Weinstein, Bernie Madoff . . .

I'll never forget the summer after my freshman year in high school. It was 1977, and the .44 Caliber Killer, aka Son of Sam, was terrorizing New York City. He killed six people before the police finally caught him. When his real name was revealed to be David Berkowitz, my mother was beside herself. "Berkowitz?!? This is the worst thing that could happen to us! I can't believe a Jewish boy would be a serial killer. They already hate us, and this is going to make it worse!" Two days later, we're eating dinner, and my mother's in a great mood. "Ma, what's with the mood swing?" (I'm sure I worded that differently, because I liked to finish my dinner.) She said, "Well, you know David Berkowitz, the Son of Sam? ADOPTED!!"

Okay, on with what this chapter's really about: my idol, Joan Rivers. The funniest and most fearless of women, Joan used words like no one else. She's included on many lists of Jewish women who changed the world. As for Judaism's speech laws, well, Joan pretty much broke them all. For that, I loved her.

There's no disputing that Joan was a pioneer. Her work and life continue to inspire and encourage comedians, and undoubtedly will for a long time. There's also no disputing that her career was, at least in some small part, made possible by the legacy of a few other brave and talented Jewish women. These stand-up ladies carved out niches for themselves in the chronically masculine—and routinely misogynistic—field of comedy.

FANNY BRICE

Men always fall for frigid women because they put on the best show.

—

You think beautiful girls are going to stay in style forever? I should say not! Any minute now they're going to be out! Finished! Then it'll be my turn!

—

Any woman who can't say a four-letter word sometimes is deceitful.

JEAN CARROLL

Oh, the way they dress down there in Florida! One woman came in with a silver fox down to her knees and a bald-headed wolf up to her chin.

—

You know that having a child is the greatest blessing in the world. Now I know, because I have my little girl. My mother kept telling me what a wonderful thing it was to be a mother. Finally came the big day in my life, I had my baby. Oh, I was so happy, I couldn't wait to send her to camp.

—

This one woman, she said she had a daughter and no matter what she did, this child just wouldn't keep a neat room. She said she tried everything—she pleaded with her, begged her, punished her, rewarded her, threatened her. Nothing she did had any effect on this child. Finally, this woman—a lot of money—she took the kid to a psychiatrist, spent thousands of dollars. You know what they found out? The kid's a slob.

BELLE BARTH

I always say, the most difficult thing for a woman to do is to try to act naive on the first night of her second marriage. She hollers, "It hurts me!" He's gotta tie his feet to the bed, he shouldn't fall in and drown.

———

One hooker says to another, "I made $150 last night."

The other asks, "Gross?"

The first replies, "No, Schwartz."

———

A woman went to the psychiatrist. The doctor says, "What's your problem?"

She says, "I got four homes, I got six Cadillacs, I got forty-two furs."

The doctor says, "What's your problem?"

She says, "My husband only makes sixty bucks a week."

———

True story about a guy who had an obsession. He hated girls all his life because, since he's a little boy, his father told him that girls have teeth on their little *pudende*. That's Italian. So, he grew up, he finally met a girl, he fell in love with her, he married her. On the wedding night he went to sleep in the living room. So, she called him, she said, "What are you, crazy? Don't you know when you get married there are certain duties a husband has to perform?"

"Aw," he says, "I love you, honey, but since I'm a little boy my father told me it's got teeth on it."

She says, "Teeth! Whaddya, crazy! Come here, I'll show you." So, she showed him. He took a look.

She said, "Does it have teeth?"

He says, "How can you have teeth when your gums are so bad?"

PEARL WILLIAMS

The definition of INDECENT: If it's long enough, hard enough, and in far enough—it's in decent.

—

Two broads are passing a beauty parlor. One says to the other, "Gee, I think I smell hair burning."
    The other one says. "Maybe we're walking a little too fast."

—

A whore goes to a bank to change a $20 bill.
    The teller says, "Miss, this is counterfeit."
    She says, "My God, I've been raped!"

TOTIE FIELDS

I've been on a diet for two weeks and all I've lost is fourteen days.

—

I exercise daily to keep my figure. I keep patting my hand against the bottom of my chin. It works, too. I have the thinnest fingers in town.

—

Happiness is a ninety-year-old man marrying an eighteen-year-old girl—because he has to.

—

My husband has not spoken to me on a football weekend in five years, other than, "Shhh." We have two kids that were born on a football weekend. One's called "Shhh" and the other's called "Get me a beer."

These were brash, outspoken women, speaking loudly, speaking angrily, and always needing to know where their children were . . . just in case.

Joan Rivers always focused on the funny, but if you were to really analyze where her humor came from, you'd immediately recognize the pain. She'd had enough of the bullshit—the double standards and hypocrisy of women's social "norms." I focus on her in particular because she wasn't only a genius, but she performed stand-up from 1959 until her sudden death in 2014. Over those fifty-five years, we made a lot of progress in our country with regard to what women couldn't, shouldn't, or wouldn't say.

In 1959, most female comics, except for some of the remarkable ladies mentioned earlier, spoke only about domestic life. A lot of material was self-deprecating, because in order to get an audience to like them, women first had to acknowledge that they knew their place and exactly what objectified pieces of shit they were. Remember that being ladylike meant to be quiet and opinionless about important issues such as business or politics—even when women were the focus of a specific policy or piece of legislation. Women weren't expected, let alone encouraged, to voice their aspirations outside marriage, motherhood, and the few professions open to them. They certainly weren't supposed to talk about their bodies and sex lives—especially onstage or on camera. Fuck that.

Joan was brilliant, her opinions were insightful. She graduated Phi Beta Kappa from Barnard College with a double major in English literature and anthropology. When you really think about it, anthropology is the basis for much of stand-up comedy. One of Joan's earlier jokes—"Education? I spit on education. No man is ever going to put his hand up your dress looking for a library card!"—says so much about the role of women in society at the time: you're useless unless you have a man. Men laughed at this joke for a very different reason than women did, but the real reason to laugh is because it's funny and true. Sadly, for some, it remains true to this day.

Early in her career, when Joan was honing her craft in Greenwich Village, she saw Lenny Bruce onstage using whatever language he wanted. He was a truth-teller, and Joan took to him immediately. One night, after he saw Joan have a bad set, he left her a note saying, "You're right and they're wrong." She kept that note in her bra up until she appeared on *The Tonight Show* and Johnny Carson told her she was going to be a star.

Joan never subscribed to the notion that women couldn't talk about certain topics. She knew that the more honest she was, the funnier she was. In an early television performance, she quipped, "A lot of people thought I wouldn't get married because . . . I don't know how many of you here are in show business, but it's very hard to meet anybody in the business because everybody you meet is either married already, or a dancer." She did a gay joke on TV! In the early '60s! Can you imagine being a closeted gay man and hearing yourself being acknowledged on national television? Joan never shied away from real life—she brought it onstage with her:

I was talking about having an affair with a married professor and that wasn't a thing a nice Jewish girl talked about. And I was talking about my mother, desperate to get my sister and me married. I was talking about my gay friend, Mr. Phyllis, and you just didn't talk about that. It sounds so tame and silly now, but my act spoke to women who weren't able to talk about things. How nice it was to have a girl that's fairly attractive stand up and say, "My mother wants me to get married, but I don't want to," or "I hated this date."

I imagine that for many women watching at the time, it was a relief to hear someone saying exactly what was going through their minds. Joan professed, until the day she died, that she said the things everyone was thinking but were too afraid to say. That's precisely what good comedians do, but even today, the stakes for women are higher than for men. If footage emerged of a female candidate for political office saying, "I just grab 'em by the balls and start kissing them. I can't help it," where would her career be now? She'd be slut-shamed, vilified, and left for dead. But when a man says that, it's dismissed as "just locker room talk," and he becomes president of the United States (unless, he indeed says "balls" instead of "pussy," in which case a whole other double standard applies).

As the times changed, so did Joan's act. Her material became a barometer of where women stood in society at the time. "Why should I clean? Housework is futile. You make the bed, you do the dishes, six months later you have to start all over again . . . When it's really filthy I call up his mother, 'Show me once more how he likes it.'"

In 1968, Joan worked as a "girl writer" on *The Beautiful Phyllis Diller Show*. The sitcom was short-lived and so was Joan's job—the program was canceled three days after she started. Phyllis Diller mentored Joan, as Joan recalled in an op-ed for the *Washington Post*: "If you wanted to be successful as a stand-up, she told me, you had to have a different, unique point of view. 'Figure out who you are, what makes you stand out from the others,' she counseled. 'The minute you know that, your comedy will fall into place. You will be able to make people laugh at things that others can't.'"[1]

During Phyllis's era, women who looked funny got more laughs, which is why Phyllis always dressed a little crazy onstage. Women had to work twice as hard to get an audience's attention, and sometimes still do. I had the good fortune to interview Phyllis. She told me that she thought her legs were funny-looking, so she always wore a short dress onstage so that everyone could see them. It made me sad.

She explained, "And the reason I developed things like [wearing a bag dress] was because I had such a great figure. So, I had to dress so that they couldn't see *any* figure, because I wanted to make jokes. I had 'em convinced that underneath whatever I was wearing, I was a skeleton, an ugly skeleton—and that's what I wanted. My legs were really thin. Model thin. I stuck out what was thin and covered up what wasn't, and everyone thought I was flat-chested."

In the '70s, Joan performed on *The Carol Burnett Show,* where she also spoke about being flat-chested. She even urged the audience to look at her chest. "On my wedding night, my husband said, 'Let me help you with the buttons,' and I said, 'I'm naked.'" She was talking about her breasts on national TV! Can you imagine these bullshit pious evangelicals hearing that material today? She also talked about marriage from a woman's perspective. One of my faves was a joke about how passion fades once you're married, how at the beginning, you're running around playing catch me! "'Catch me, catch me!' I'm married nine years, we still play catch me, but we walk. [*slowly*] 'Catch me, catch me.' 'Can I catch you tomorrow?' 'Sure! Tomorrow's even better, I'll know in advance, I'll shave my legs.'"

Joan even goes on to joke about the difference between a first wife and a second wife, and how men like the second wife so much better because they're cute and shallow. These were women's issues—getting dumped for someone younger, aging, divorce, sex, going to the gynecologist, childbirth. You name it, Joan wrote a joke about it. All the stuff women were whispering about on the phone to their friends or gossiping about at their bridge club—she put it all out there. Yes, some considered it raunchy, but Joan was unapologetic. She owned her material just like the guy comics did, but she did it in a dress. She never toned down her femininity. As a teenage girl living in the New Jersey suburbs, I picked up on the message she was sending: It's okay to talk about the elephant in the room. In fact, it's mandatory (especially if the elephant in the room is you). You don't have to avoid discussions because someone might be uncomfortable. If they are—even better! As Joan once put it, "A man can sleep around, no questions asked. But if a woman makes nineteen or twenty mistakes, she's a tramp."

As much as Joan was breaking the mold with her irreverence, the world was being run by men (and still is). At the networks, men decided what television shows America watched. Looking back, it seems uncanny that a nondescript white gentile named Johnny Carson took to Joan's humor in such a huge way. There was Carson, a Midwestern man, guffawing at this petite Jewish woman as she audaciously broke every rule about how women were supposed to behave and which topics were appropriate for her to broach. Keep in mind that when Joan started doing stand-up, CBS wouldn't permit their biggest star, Lucille Ball, a pregnant woman playing a pregnant character, to use the word *pregnant* on air.

By the late 1970s and into the 1980s, Joan was a veritable star who made fun of everyone. Her jokes about Elizabeth Taylor's weight were relentless.

She puts mayonnaise on aspirin.

—

She pierced her ears and gravy ran out.

—

Mosquitoes see her and scream, "Buffet!"

When people reacted disapprovingly to Joan's "fat shaming," she joked about their reactions: "That's it! I will not do any more

Liz Taylor jokes. No more!!! I'm leaving the poor woman alone . . .
I bet you're all saying, 'Yeah, right, FAT chance'!"

Joan was absofuckinglutely hilarious when she made fun of
people. She was one of the small number of comedians who could
get away with it, along with Don Rickles, Jeff Ross, Robert Smigel
(aka Triumph the Insult Comic Dog), and Lisa Lampanelli. Frequently, comedians just starting out will think that insults will
get them laughs. They come out swinging at the audience or attacking celebrities, only to discover that the crowd thinks they're
pathetic losers. Why is it that insulting people worked so well
for Joan? She, along with a few others, was gifted with a quality that my pal Eddie Sarfaty calls "the caustic warmth." People
were willing to laugh along with Joan because they could tell that
underneath the stinging barbs, there was a generous, kind human
being. (Eddie's told me that I also have that quality, but he's a
fucking asshole who ate all my Klondike bars, so . . .)

And while I'm on the subject, I want to point out something
important. Earlier in this book, I wrote about the problem of
people getting offended by jokes taken out of context—when
hearing them told secondhand or when reading them in print.
But context isn't limited to text; it also includes the manner in
which the joke is told: the inflection in the comedian's voice,
their body language, their facial expressions, the words they
emphasize—in short, the emotion behind the line. Joan's words
were often vicious, but her respect and affection for the audience
was always apparent.

Joan wasn't heartless. She asked actor Roddy McDowall, a
friend she and Liz Taylor had in common, if the fat jokes were
bothering Taylor, and told him that if they were, she'd stop telling them. Taylor said to Roddy, "Tell your friend Joan Rivers it
doesn't bother me where I live." Really? Really? Tell that to Don-

ald Trump. Joan had a joke about Willie Nelson. Because he and his band had a reputation for being grungy, she mocked him, saying that "he wore a roach motel around his neck." Nelson's daughter personally wrote to Joan to tell her that because of her joke, she was getting made fun of in school. The joke immediately came out of Joan's repertoire.[2]

In May 1987, Joan's career came to a screeching halt. She'd been a favorite guest of Carson's through the years, and in 1983 she'd officially become his permanent guest host. As Carson was approaching his twenty-fifth year of hosting *The Tonight Show,* NBC anticipated that he would soon retire. When a list of his possible replacements was leaked, Joan found out her name wasn't on it. So when Fox extended an offer for her to host her own late-night show, Joan accepted. When she called to tell Carson, he hung up on her! They never spoke again.

Joan hosted *The Late Show Starring Joan Rivers* for a little over seven months before she was fired. Three months after that, her husband Edgar Rosenberg committed suicide. It was the perfect storm. Joan had basically lost everything. (And by the way, if you think the fact that Joan was a woman had nothing to do with Carson's rejection, you're 100 percent wrong. Several of Carson's male guests went on to host their own shows and he didn't give a shit.) Joan wouldn't do late-night for another twenty-one years.

After Edgar's death, Joan couldn't get a job; no one wanted her. She found herself in her fifties back in the clubs where she'd started. What was she talking about onstage? Take a wild guess.

My husband killed himself and it was my fault. We were making love and I took the bag off my head.

My husband wanted to be cremated. I told him I'd scatter
his ashes at Neiman Marcus—that way, I'd visit him every day.

There was no "too soon" with Joan; this was hers to talk
about. Even if people felt uncomfortable, there was no way she'd
ever let an elephant steal the audience's focus.

In 1989, Joan was given her own daytime talk show, and she
was daring even in daytime. The thing I remember most was how
she booked gay people and drag queens during the height of the
AIDS crisis and treated them with the utmost respect. In 1990 she
won the Emmy for Best Daytime Talk Show Host. It was a well-
deserved validation from the business that had shunned her. She
cherished that Emmy because they could never take it away from
her. In her speech, she mentioned how Edgar had always told her,
"You can always turn things around." Unfortunately, the depth of
his despair prevented him from taking his own advice.

I'm sure most people remember the last two decades of Joan's
career the best. She practically created the red carpet, and in turn
defended her right to free speech. She used phrases like "Oh,
come on!" "Grow up!" and, my favorite, "You know what I'm
talking about!" (That last one makes me ponder whether she was
giving the audience way more credit than they deserved.) During an awards season wrap-up episode of *Fashion Police*, Joan
made a comment about Heidi Klum, who was wearing a gold dress
that exposed large portions of her body. "The last time a German
looked this hot was when they were pushing Jews into the ovens." Okay, that is darkly hilarious.

There was utter outrage from the Anti-Defamation League
(ADL) as well as from other organizations and individuals. Utter
outrage! But here's the deal: Germans DID push Jews into ovens.

It's a fact. It actually happened. And Heidi Klum is German. She's also hot—and was especially so that night. What Joan did was bring together two completely different meanings of the word *hot* and simultaneously remind the world of the Holocaust. Edgar had lost much of his family in the Holocaust. It was a fucking joke, and a funny one.

Joan never worried that she was minimizing or dismissing the horrors of the Holocaust; in fact, she thought quite the opposite. She trusted that gassing fellow human beings and burning them in ovens was evil and abominable to most people. She was confident that telling a joke about it wasn't suddenly going to persuade people that it wasn't. And if you're one of those inbred racist assholes who tortured animals as a child and thinks a swastika makes your micro penis look bigger, she knew she wasn't going to change your mind anyway. Another thing—if you've studied the Holocaust, you know for a fact that there were Jews making jokes, clowning around, and laughing to allow themselves a few moments to feel human despite the savagely cruel conditions and crushing terror under which they were living.

Who decided that making a joke about a disaster is wicked and immoral? There's not only one acceptable way to speak about something horrific; if you speak about a tragedy delicately, it doesn't make discussing the tragedy more palatable. Hearing a joke about the Holocaust or the Great Depression or Pearl Harbor or the assassination of Martin Luther King Jr. or the space shuttle *Challenger* or 9/11 or Hurricane Katrina isn't going to strip away your knowledge or your empathy.

And why, in our society, do some people think it's okay for them to dictate what jokes are appropriate for others? It's called a *sense* of humor for a reason; it's subjective. Each individual member of the audience gets to decide if what they're hearing is inappropriate or offensive. If they feel it is, they don't have to laugh. If they're watching at home, they can change the channel or turn the television off. If they're at a live performance, they can boo or hiss or just get up and walk out the fucking door.

Joan Rivers had an FBI file. Over the course of her career, she made a few enemies and received two death threats. After telling a few Polish jokes at the Deauville Beach Resort in Miami in 1973, she received a Western Union telegram from an offended audience member as well as threatening phone calls. Not much seems to have changed since then, and because of social media, it's gotten way worse. It's so much easier for jokes to get taken out of context or retold by the offended party to fit their agenda. You know what a comic's agenda is? To make people laugh. That's all.

On July 1, 2014, Joan's twelfth book, *Diary of a Mad Diva,* hit bookstores. Four days later, Joan went on CNN to promote it and was interviewed by Fredricka Whitfield. Do yourself a favor and watch the interview. Whitfield bombarded Joan with negative question after negative question. She remarked on Joan's decision to wear fur on the book's cover. She called Joan's fashion critiques mean. "It's not mean," Joan responded. "I tell the truth. I'm sure I say the same things that your viewers say to their friends sitting next to them on the couch." Whitfield went on to ask Joan, "Do you feel like there are boundaries, ever?" Joan responded, "Lemme tell you, life is very tough and if you can make a joke to make something easier and funny, do it. Done."

Joan was there to talk about her book, not to defend herself. Whitfield should have thanked her for coming on the show, not harassed her. Before Joan got up and stormed out of the interview, she told Whitfield, "I have made people laugh for fifty years. I am put on Earth to make people laugh. My book is funny. I wear fur that was killed fifteen years ago. I work for animal rights. Stop it with, 'and you do this, and you're mean, and you're that.' You're not the person to interview someone that does humor. Sorry."

Joan would die a mere eight weeks after that interview. She fought for the respect she deserved right up until the very end, and when she was gone, her fans picked up the slack. Joan was a massive supporter of the arts. Whenever possible, she attended Broadway, Off-Broadway, and Off-Off-Broadway opening nights. She appeared on Broadway and, in 1994, was nominated for a Tony Award. When a theater luminary dies, the Broadway League dims the lights of Broadway theaters in tribute, but they refused to dim the lights for Joan until a storm of outrage on social media forced them to change their minds.

Joan was also left out of the Oscars' "In Memoriam" segment that year, even though she'd appeared in, written, and directed several films and been a fixture at the awards for years interviewing celebrities on the red carpet. The Academy defended itself by saying Joan was included in the Academy's online "In Memoriam" gallery. Really? The only reason half the television audience watched the Oscars was to see what Joan had to say. And FYI, if the ratings continue going in the direction they've been going, the only way anyone's going to be able to see the Academy Awards is online.

I cried a lot when Joan died. I lost my comedy godmother. I'd known who she was since I could talk. I watched her every time she was on TV and memorized her albums. I adored her. A couple of months before her death, I got to spend time with her backstage in between her shows at Town Hall in Provincetown, Massachusetts. I'll never forget her asking me to make a Vine video. "A Vine video?" I had no idea what she was talking about. She was always up to date on things and attuned to what was on people's minds. She knew everything about pop culture and was never more hip or relevant than she was at eighty-one.

I attended Joan's memorial service. I laughed hard and cried hard, too. People from every part of her life praised her. Howard Stern spoke about how he wouldn't be where he is today without Joan. In an interview with the *Hollywood Reporter,* Chris Rock said, "Joan Rivers is one of the greatest stand-up comedians to ever live." He went on: "She was the hippest comedian from the time she started to the day she died. So, don't put Joan Rivers in a box, because she's like Mount Rushmore."[3]

Joan was an iconoclast. Nothing was sacred. She loved to rip apart the royal family:

> Oh, grow up! Prince Charles is gay. He can't wait for the mother to die, so he can become queen!
>
> ⸺
>
> Do you find them good-looking, the royal family? 'Cause my husband's English—he thinks they're good-looking. Can we talk here? A bunch of dogs. A bunch of dogs! Go out in the street, call their names, "Queenie, Duke, and Prince!" See what shows up.
>
> ⸺
>
> I think my husband had an affair with the queen of England. He never said so, but he was out one night in London, he came home with tiara marks all over his stomach.

It might surprise you to know that Joan and Prince Charles were friends—good friends. She was one of only four Americans invited to his 2005 wedding to Camilla Parker Bowles, and she performed at a gala for his sixtieth birthday. When she died, Charles put out a statement saying, "Joan Rivers was an extraordinary woman with an original and indefatigable spirit, an unstoppable sense of humor and an enormous zest for life. She will be hugely missed and utterly irreplaceable."[4] If the heir to the British throne, raised in the most genteel society, schooled in royal etiquette, and sensitive to the slightest breach of decorum, can take a joke, then so can you.

"We don't apologize for a joke," Joan said. "We are comics. We are here to make you laugh. If you don't get it, then don't watch us." I admire Joan's ferocity in this statement, but if you'll allow, I'd like to make one small clarification. We don't apologize for GOOD jokes. They're what we're supposed to bring to the stage. The only way to make a joke good is to take it to the edge, and sometimes we need to go over the edge to find out exactly where the edge lies. Regrettably, during the process, we can unintentionally cause someone pain. Comics are human, and we make mistakes, but there's a thing called forgiveness, which is the necessary ingredient to put things into perspective and move on with our lives.

Fanny Brice, Pearl Williams, Totie Fields, and the other pioneering Jewish female comedians readied the world for Joan Rivers. In addition to giving birth to her daughter ("Melissa, you ripped me to shreds—go back to sleep."), Joan, in her fearlessness and tenacity, engendered generations of gut-busting female stand-ups, including:

ELAYNE BOOSLER

I do clean up a little if company is coming; I'll wipe the lipstick off the milk container.

———

My mother always said you could eat off her floor. You could eat off my floor, too—there's so much food down there.

———

Men put all kinds of expectations on you. They want you to scream, "You're the best," while swearing you've never done this with anyone before.

SUSIE ESSMAN

Men are simple and women are complex. It's a fact. We love you guys, but we love you in a patronizing way. Like kinda how you love the village idiot.

—

I'm single. My friends tell me I should get one of those mechanical devices. I've never used one because I'm too scared—because they say they're so fabulous. I think, "What if it's so fabulous? You use it, you get addicted, you have to move on to bigger and better appliances?" You find yourself leaning against the dishwasher ever so slightly. One day your boyfriend walks in. He finds you riding the Maytag screaming, "Spin cycle, spin cycle, SPIN CYCLE!"

—

This guy out of nowhere just says to me, "SLUT!" I was so appalled. Let me tell you, I got up off my knees and I marched out of that stall with my dignity intact. And every other guy in that bathroom knew that I was a lady.

RITA RUDNER

I love being married. It's so great to find that one special person you want to annoy for the rest of your life.

—

Marriages don't last. When I meet a guy, the first question I ask myself is: Is this the man I want my children to spend their weekends with?

—

Some people think having large breasts makes a woman stupid. Actually, it's quite the opposite: a woman having large breasts makes men stupid.

—

My husband and I are either going to buy a dog or have a child. We can't decide whether to ruin our carpet or ruin our lives.

ROSEANNE BARR

As a housewife, I feel that if the kids are still alive when my husband gets home from work, then hey, I've done my job.

CATHY LADMAN

Makeup is such a weird concept. I'll wake up in the morning and look in the mirror. "Gee, I really don't look so good. Maybe if my eyelids were blue, I'd be more attractive."

—

My parents only had one argument in forty-five years. It lasted forty-three years.

—

I got a postcard from my gynecologist. It said, "Did you know it's time for your annual checkup?" No, but now my mailman does.

CAROL LEIFER

The only thing I said to my parents when I was a teenager was, "Hang up, I got it!"

—

Making love to a woman is like buying real estate: location, location, location.

—

I was working recently in London—what a thrill, yeah. But
I wasn't used to their money, though, 'cause I bought
this really decadent box of chocolates—the cashier said,
"That'll be ten pounds." I'm like, "Rub it in, why don't you?"

SUE KOLINSKY

People love to heckle comedians. Stand-up comedy is the
only profession where people pay to come see you and
then try to prevent you from doing your job. You wouldn't
go to your accountant and try to mess him up while he
was doing your taxes. Pull the plug out while he's adding.
Get into his face: 8, 4, 7 . . .

I read an article in a magazine: women forty-nine years
old having their first child. Forty-nine! I couldn't think
of a better way to spend my golden years. What's the
advantage of having a kid at forty-nine? So you can both
be in diapers at the same time?

WENDY LIEBMAN

I've been on so many blind dates, I should get a free dog.

I didn't know what to wear . . . obviously. I never know what
to wear. I got an obscene phone call and the guy was like,
"What are you wearing? What are you wearing?" And I'm
like, "I can't decide. Hello? Hello?" He got off . . . the phone.

I am reading some fiction right now. It's called *The Joy of
Cooking.*

JACKIE HOFFMAN

I grew up listening to records of Broadway musicals and memorizing them. By the time I was nine years old, I was a gay man.

—

I won't adopt a child because it would interfere with my career . . . oh, and there's one more reason. What was it? Oh yeah . . . I hate them.

SARAH SILVERMAN

I was raped by a doctor. Which is, you know, so bittersweet for a Jewish girl.

(Sarah will not do this joke anymore. I think it's perfect. Sorry, Sarah.)

I was licking jelly off of my boyfriend's penis and all of a sudden I'm thinking, "Oh my God, I'm turning into my mother!"

—

I don't care if you think I'm racist. I just want you to think I'm thin.

CORY KAHANEY

I have a husband, he's nice, people like him. Everybody always wants to know where we met—they think I've got the secret. I hate to tell the secret—I met my husband in a bar. Generally, girls know that's not a good idea. It's like going grocery shopping when you're hungry and you bring home stuff you don't need.

OPHIRA EISENBERG

My husband called me passive-aggressive. I told him to go screw himself. In an email. Saved as a draft. But he'll find it.

———

I'm still in my first marriage—that's horrible, that's awful. I shouldn't talk about it like that, so temporary . . . My current husband hates when I do that.

AMY SCHUMER

My mom's always saying really smart things. Like, you probably heard this one: "Why buy the cow when the milk has HPV?" Wish I'd listened to that one.

———

You feel like such a dirty whore buying Plan B. It's so embarrassing because it's over-the-counter but you have to ask your pharmacist, and they know what you want but they make you ask. They're lookin' at me, I'm like, "You see where my eyeliner is, just give it to me."

There are many other hilarious Jewish women such as Michele Balan, Jessica Kirson, and Rachel Feinstein, who make audiences laught night after night.

Without Joan—if she'd been shut down—the voices of these brilliant women, and women of all religions, colors, shapes, and sizes, might never have been heard. And that would have been a tragedy.

11

Fuck You, Mark Zuckerberg

If you stand on a soapbox and trade
rhetoric with a dictator, you never win.

—MEL BROOKS

I have a love–hate relationship with social media. Mostly hate. For a comedian like myself, it's a necessary evil, a colossal waste of time, and a great way to promote your shows and let your fans know you're not dead yet. It's also disturbingly easy to get sucked into the vortex of watching a cat video, and then another, and another, and another. And let me tell you something: if I see one more person post a photo of themselves in the ICU, with an oxygen mask strapped on their face and tubes coming out of them, an IV pole, and wearing a hospital gown, and the caption beneath the photo reads, "Wish me luck," I'm going to fucking kill myself! And these people never tell you what's wrong with them! Are you getting a heart transplant or a face-lift? How much attention do you need? You know what Facebook is? Munchausen syndrome.

So many things about social media drive me crazy. I hate when people post photos of their food. Why do you have to advertise the meal you made? Isn't it simply enough to have a nice dinner with your family? Why do you need random people "liking" you? Another thing, I have all these friends who are in horrible relationships. They call me every day saying, "I hate her so much. She's verbally abusive. I feel like I'm in prison. The minute I have enough money, I'm out of here!" Then, thirty minutes later, I'll go on Facebook and see a picture of them together with the caption,

"Happy Birthday to the love of my life. You are my everything!" Social media outlets like Facebook, Twitter, Instagram, and Snapchat allow people to portray a perfect life that, sadly, they're not living.

I must admit that virtual reality's truly amazing. Without getting off the sofa, a prospective student can tour a college thousands of miles away; during a coffee break, a potential homeowner can attend an open house in another state; and, if you own a StairMaster and the right goggles, you can climb Mount Everest without ever leaving your garage. But just as reality television has little to nothing to do with reality, enjoying the technological wonders of virtual reality is no substitute for real experiences, in real places, in real time, with real people. In virtual reality, you might get an essence of the thrill of an experience, but until someone perfects a way to deceive our entire nervous system (which will probably happen much sooner than we think), there are no odors, no tastes, and nothing tactile. Your "adventure" is simply not genuine. The same thing's true about comedy. Whenever I'm fighting with my kids or my girlfriend over a misread text, I'm certain there'd have been no misconceptions if we'd spoken in person or even over the phone. Comedy's one of those things that can only be communicated accurately in a specific way. It's another reason why comics get in trouble.

As you know by now, there's nothing new about any of this. Audiences have always found things some comedians say offensive and have subsequently pushed back. They've protested, written letters, made phone calls, boycotted businesses, written op-eds, etc.

Comedians have been banned, called out by politicians and the media, denounced by churches and civil organizations, blacklisted, fired, and forever vilified. Nevertheless, we've persisted.

Though engaged in a perpetual tug-o'-war, society and comedy have pushed each other forward, and hopefully will forever do so. Unfortunately, today the tension's been magnified exponentially by the advent of social media.

Even the beneficial aspects of social media have a downside. These platforms give comedians way more exposure than was previously possible, and those with wider exposure can attract larger audiences, which means greater profits for clubs and comics alike. Yet veteran stand-up comics—solid performers who've spent years building a following and perfecting their acts—can lose gigs to younger, less experienced (and often unfunny) novices because some producers are less concerned with talent than with how many followers a comedian has. For those of us who did all the right things to become successful and well respected, it can feel like a punch in the gut to discover that the rules have changed. Under the new rules, all the time we spend writing and living (what's there to write about if you've got no life?) to generate quality material has to be curtailed so we can create content (in 280 characters or less), which, once posted, sparks reactions that take over our lives. Don't forget, stand-ups are used to instant gratification. Since we can't hear a laugh or a groan through our smartphones or computers, we keep checking and checking to see if we've gotten a decent reaction. And because everybody else on the planet is using the same apps as us, it's as if they're also getting a chance at the mic. The moment someone logs in, their soapbox is waiting, and the moral outrage commences. Now you know why they call them social media *platforms*.

Moral outrage plus social media can obliterate a comedian's career. Not only can a comedian get called out by someone in the audience in response to a joke, but that audience member can tweet or post the instant they're offended, at the height of their outrage, before they have time to cool down or reconsider. Their rant hits the cloud and goes viral, causing damage far greater than was possible in the past. And, as I noted previously, due to the limits of the platform, not to mention the inadequacy of the written word to convey everyday multisensorial experiences, the message generated is distorted, devoid of nuance, tone, and intent. Take the last fight you had with your spouse via text or email (caps and all), multiply that by thousands, and you can see how much harm can be done to a comedian's career. Furthermore, when an audience member records, without permission, video or audio of a comic's performance and posts a portion of it online, completely out of context, it can derail a comedian's career for years. Even the tiniest onstage errors, perceived or real, are now exposed for condemnation. Imagine someone recording your every move at work, and the one time you fuck up, they post the video online for everyone to see. Like other professionals, comedians want the opportunity to put their best foot forward and not have their image reduced to their worst moments. Everybody has bad days at work that they'd rather forget.

Pretty much all comedy venues prohibit audience members from recording anything, but because some people think they're above the rules, video and audio of comedians' works-in-progress turn up online. Sometimes a joke's not working yet because one word is wrong. At other times, the subject matter is risky and the comic hasn't quite figured out how to make it palatable enough yet. It can take a long time and a lot of repetition to fine-tune a setup or punch line. Think of the scope and reach of the internet, and you'll see how, when some asshole decides to share a comic's unfinished work, it can sabotage the development of material.

It's as if you're writing a novel, but before you have a chance to proofread or edit it, someone forwards copies to every newspaper, periodical, and website to review.

In 2016, Margaret Cho opened her set at a club in New Brunswick, New Jersey, doing a bit about race and rape. Margaret's the daughter of Korean immigrants and grew up in an extremely diverse area of San Francisco. As a child, not only was she bullied for her body, her round face, and her ethnicity, she was also sexually molested and raped starting at the age of five. That is her truth, and she's been very outspoken about it—so naturally, it's part of her stand-up. (Remember, you can make a joke about any topic as long as the joke is funny.)

Some members of the audience became so incensed by her material, that, before walking out of the show, they went up to the stage and screamed at her. That's not a common occurrence in comedy clubs. Of course, there's always the possibility of a heckler of two, but for the most part, the comedian puts them in their places and moves on. This was different. The club management and the police had to intervene.

Afterward, Margaret wrote an apology on the club's Facebook page:

> I'm sorry that I wasn't at my best, but maybe in a way,
> I was. I bring the real me and my truth to my work. It's
> not perfect, it's not manufactured, it's real. Everyone has
> a bad day at work. I was also upset because one of my
> heroes (Garry Shandling) just died. That doesn't excuse my
> behavior, but it just shows that I am only human.

Her effort to make things better didn't end there. A few months after the experience, Margaret appeared on Jerry Seinfeld's show *Comedians in Cars Getting Coffee*. Jerry and Margaret talked about that specific night, and during their discussion, they had an idea. What if Margaret invited the audience back to the club, facilitated a discussion, and performed another set? That's exactly what happened. They picked a date and sent out invitations. The audience arrived at the club early, and they had a discussion—comic and spectators. After the talk, they took a break and then did a show, with Jerry opening for Margaret.

I spoke with Margaret, curious about how she felt about that experience a few years later. She told me she was very glad she went back. "I'm really happy that I got to resolve it. Sometimes those nights stick in your head forever, and the trauma is reignited later over and over. I'm so relieved it's all forgiven in every aspect and turned into something very transformative." I asked Margaret if any of this would have happened had the original incident not been recorded and posted on social media. "It's two separate schools of thought, and yes, nobody would have cared except for video." I agree with her 100 percent.

She went on: "It's really a shame-based culture we live in today. People love to use videos on social media as a kind of governing body of a collective moral compass." I respect Margaret's candor. It saddens me that what happens inside a comedy club, a comedian's home, can be taken out of context and preserved that way for posterity.

Finally, I asked if she had learned anything from the experience, and she replied, "I think it's just to listen to people more and to remain teachable in the way that comedy is. I am more respectful toward the audience in a way, and also harder on them, too. It made me a better comic." And I must tell you, she was already a damn good comic to begin with. Thankfully Margaret didn't lose work over this.

As I mentioned earlier, Gilbert Gottfried lost his job with Aflac for being Gilbert. On his way home from a gig in Philly, his agent called and asked him to lay off tweeting about the tsunami because Aflac was not happy. Fine. But his agent didn't say anything to Gilbert about being fired. Gilbert found out exactly the way the rest of us did—on the internet. When he got home, he turned on his computer and there it was! Top story. How ridiculous! As Gilbert told me, "Bad taste jokes have always been around. There have been dead baby jokes forever. But those jokes have a built-in apology. When people hear them, they cringe and cover their faces as if to say, 'This is horrible and shouldn't be joked about, but I'm laughing because it's funny.'"

Joking is a coping mechanism, and one that's way better than drinking or doing drugs. A day or two after the tsunami, Gilbert turned on the news, and he remembers one news anchor reporting terrible details about the tsunami and then saying, "And to make matters worse, comedian Gilbert Gottfried . . ." "I made it worse?" Gilbert asked, incredulous. "What kind of powers do I have?"

To top it all off, Gilbert couldn't leave his apartment without being bombarded. There were cars parked outside at all hours of the day, people hiding in doorways, paparazzi and news reporters waiting for him to appear, as if he was a serial killer.

"When the top story in the news is that your career is over," Gilbert said, "you realize, if it was over, then it wouldn't be the top story." News flash!! Gilbert Gottfried did NOT make the tsunami worse. The power of the internet is quite something, isn't it? He continued, "The internet makes me feel sentimental for the old lynch mobs. They actually had to work and get their hands dirty. Now they just sit in their underwear posting on the internet." I couldn't have said it better myself.

In September 2018, Wanda Sykes was performing at the Count Basie Center for the Arts in Red Bank, New Jersey. She opened her set with a series of Trump jokes. A few Trump supporters in the audience heckled her, and about a dozen of them walked out or were asked to leave. Naturally, when the incident first appeared on Twitter, it was reported that far more than a dozen people walked out. In her comedy special *Not Normal,* Wanda opened the show by dealing with that event head-on. "If you voted for Trump, and you came to see me? [*huge applause and laughter*] You fucked up again." Just like any great comic, she got the last laugh, and that's exactly the way it should be.

My younger son and his friends' social media platform of choice is Snapchat. When you use Snapchat to send photos and messages, whatever you send is only available for viewing for a short period of time. After that, those messages are no longer accessible. My son and his friends are convinced that their posts just disappear into the ether and can never be found again. If only. There's no such thing as a fire that turns everything to ashes when we're talking about the internet. And since we are now living in a "cancel culture," where disparate, unpopular, and risqué opinions or actions from your past can be conjured up at a moment's notice and haunt you for the rest of your life, nothing is ever certain. Just ask Kevin Hart.

On a Tuesday in December 2018, it was announced that comedian Kevin Hart had been chosen to host the 2019 Academy Awards. I'm telling you right now that every single stand-up comic has dreamed of hosting the Oscars. Immediately after the announcement, the outrage began. In an old special, Kevin had talked about his fear of having a gay son. He also posted some homophobic tweets in 2009, 2010, and 2011. In one of his tweets, Kevin declared that if he caught his son playing with a dollhouse, he'd "break it over his head & say n my voice 'stop that's gay.'" Kevin had apologized for those tweets years ago, but that wasn't enough. The Academy of Motion Picture Arts and Sciences wanted him to issue another apology. He declined, because, as he said, "I've done it. I'm not going to continue to go back and tap into the days of old when I've moved on and I'm in a completely different space in my life." He went on to say, "We feed internet trolls and we reward them."

Now, a lot of my gay male friends, who were victims of physical abuse as children simply for being gay, were happy in the end that he didn't host the Oscars. I understand that the words and bits from Kevin's past were offensive and conjured up horrible things for my friends—things that LGBTQ kids deal with to this day. But as someone in the LGBTQ community, I must say that one of the major goals of our activism is to help individuals shed their homophobia and evolve into people who treat us with the respect and dignity we deserve. Kevin is a perfect example of someone who's evolved. I've known him for a long time. He's one of the nicest and kindest guys in the business. He's apologized, and he's worked his ass off to get to where he is now. He's not our enemy. We all need to move on.

Sam Seder, a comedian turned MSNBC political pundit and host of *The Majority Report,* was notified in December 2017 that MSNBC would be cutting ties with him. The alt-right—specifically, the alt-wrong social media personality, conspiracy theorist, and all-around asshole Mike Cernovich—had been circulating an old tweet of Sam's. In 2009, after Roman Polanski was arrested in Switzerland on a decades-old warrant for having intercourse with a thirteen-year-old girl in 1977, some well-known artists and celebrities argued for his release on the basis that he's a creative genius. Disgusted by this, Sam posted an obviously sarcastic tweet:

Dont care re Polanski but i hope if my daughter is ever
raped it is by an older truly talented man w/ a great sense
of mise en scene.

Clearly, Seder was mocking Polanski and his defenders, and ultimately MSNBC retracted his firing. Talk about using social media as a weapon.

I think about how lucky I was that the internet wasn't around when I was a kid getting bullied. I had the luxury of going home after school, retreating to my room, and enjoying a respite from all the crap I was dealing with by blasting my record player and singing into a hairbrush. That's no longer the case for kids who are like I was. Cyberbullying is relentless. If you have a username that starts with an @, I'd bet it's 100 percent likely that you've been bullied. Right now, a comic somewhere is being bullied into deleting a tweet that someone took offense to. It's fucking out of control! When actress Carrie Fisher died in December 2016, her good friend Steve Martin tweeted:

When I was a young man, Carrie Fisher was the most
beautiful creature I had ever seen. She turned out to be
witty and bright as well.

The backlash was immediate. Why? Some women were offended because they felt that Martin's focus was on Fisher's looks. They felt he was objectifying her. My interpretation is that he was saying that he was initially struck by her beauty and then, when he got to know her, it was her intelligence and wit that were the most striking things about her. You can't tell me that you haven't noticed someone was really hot and then were really blown away when you discovered they were also a concert pianist or a poet, or had dual PhDs in molecular biology and Slavic languages. Cut the faux outrage. It's so boring.

Social media isn't social at all, and it's certainly not a safe or friendly place for any opinionated, petulant, boundary-pushing, racist, homophobic, anti-Semitic misogynist who happens to be gainfully employed, with one exception. Donald Trump. Yet even Trump supporter Roseanne Barr lost her hit TV show *Roseanne* in May 2018, after posting this tweet about Valerie Jarrett, a senior advisor to President Obama:

Muslim brotherhood & planet of the apes had a baby=vj.

ABC immediately fired Roseanne, and as it turned out, Valerie Jarrett couldn't have given two shits about it. She was more concerned about families being separated at the border and children being shot dead in their classrooms. Someone who knows what's important in this world.

There seems to be an endless stream of apologies from comedians who want to keep their jobs. During a discussion on *The View* regarding Kelley Johnson, who competed in the Miss America 2016 pageant as Miss Colorado, the hosts weighed in on Johnson's talent presentation, in which she appeared in medical scrubs with a stethoscope around her neck and delivered a monologue about her experiences as a nurse. As the hosts were chattering, Joy Behar, obviously not clear about Johnson's profession, asked, "Why does she have a doctor's stethoscope on?"

Well, that was it!! Backlash all over the internet. Nurses everywhere were livid. How dare Joy intimate that only doctors, not nurses, use stethoscopes! They even created a hashtag on Twitter, #nursesunite, and both Johnson & Johnson and Eggland's Best pulled their advertising from *The View*. Joy apologized for being so ignorant and insensitive. Are we really this fragile?

Other comics have either been forced to apologize or had a rude awakening and finally saw the light. Bill Maher, Trevor Noah, Sarah Silverman, Tracy Morgan, and many more comics have asked for forgiveness. Even a comedian who'd moved on from the field of stand-up and become a senator fighting for the rights of women and minorities and standing on the absolute right side of history got burned by the past. We all lost when Senator Al Franken was forced to apologize and resign over some stupid joke from years ago. How long is this going to go on? What's more important, facts or feelings? You know what's funny? The fact that we wake up every single day to shit like this coming from people tweeting from the safety of their anonymous pulpits. Just for fun, here are a few of the greatest hits about me that I've received:

It's wrong to market your disgusting lifestyle to children.

———

Do you own a mirror? You're half a chromosome away from a water buffalo. Just sayin.

———

How about a mask for your hideous face.

———

Delete your account stupid bitch.

———

They should have another holocaust just for you.

———

Judy Gold is a hypocritical Jew Cunt.

THE VICIOUSNESS IS FAR GREATER than ever before in both intensity and frequency. These days, there's so much pressure on comedians—and the venues and companies that employ them—to water down, sanitize, and discard certain material to the detriment of the art of comedy. Yes, comedy is an art, not a science. And all this pressure to be milquetoast and inoffensive is like harassing Wu-Tang Clan to make an album of medieval choral music.

Believe it or not, there's a well-known working comedian who's never, ever been on social media. She doesn't even have email. Janeane Garofalo. When I asked her why, she replied, "I don't have thick skin. I do care what people think about me." She went on to say, "The more you put yourself out there, the more reason you give people to dislike you." As we talked and reminisced about life before cell phones, computers, and every other "smart" technological appendage, I began to miss the good old days. Janeane has a phone, but she doesn't have anyone's information in it. When she picks up a call and says hello, she has no idea who's on the other end. Do you remember those days when someone picked up the telephone, heard your voice, and was genuinely surprised and happy to hear from you? Can you even recall that feeling? Our children will never experience that. I felt a bit jealous of Janeane's freedom, but she pointed out that things would be different if she had kids. She writes everything down using pen and paper. I guess you could call her the Amish-ish comedian. She told me that, "When the grid goes down, and it will, a lot of people will go insane. It'll just be a Tuesday to me." Lucky her.

Conclusion

So, What the Hell Are We Gonna Do About It?

Life is too short to be taken seriously.

—OSCAR WILDE

Thank God Don Rickles is dead. Known as one of the most thoughtful, kind, and generous guys in the business, he was the insult comic with a huge heart. I shudder to think how he and his act would fare in this PC culture. Political correctness is a virus that's killing great stand-up comedy, and that, in turn, is killing us all. Political correctness was invented to avoid insulting marginalized groups of people. I'm all for it! I hear it works very well in the office. As I've noted, I'd probably last about an hour in an office environment

Political correctness and great comedy are mutually exclusive. Comedy has been around since the first ape slipped on a banana peel; political correctness, maybe fifty years. The first joke ever recorded was a fart joke. Yet after millennia of human civilization, there are still far too many people inconsolably outraged by anecdotes about bodily functions that it begs the question of whether we've evolved at all.

So many of the great trailblazers mentioned in this book would be bullied into silence by internet trolls if they ever came back to life. If people spent the same amount of time listening to some great stand-up comedy on their huge headphones as they do posting selfies and pontificating about meaningless bullshit, the world would be a joyous place. Laughter is an integral part of a happy and fulfilling life. Look on any dating site and you'll see I'm right.

The most important attribute when seeking a potential mate: a sense of humor.

What's that, Judy?

A SENSE OF HUMOR!

Thank you.

To my fellow comedians, I say, "We need to stop apologizing unnecessarily." There are a few creative geniuses who've never apologized and rightly so—Lewis Black, Ricky Gervais, Chris Rock, and Sacha Baron Cohen. Follow their leads. The battles fought by those before us were not for nothing. They paved the way. Stay on the path.

In this book, I've stated that as comedians, we should use stereotypes appropriately. When we use potentially loaded language, we should do so judiciously and precisely. We should refrain from maliciously offending people. We should demonstrate our willingness to laugh at ourselves. And, we should endeavor to gain the audience's trust.

There's a lot that clubs and theaters can do to help bring back the good old days. They can insist on phone-free audiences—it's happening more and more. In fact, at the Comedy Cellar in New York City, audience members are required to turn off their phones and put them in sealed pouches before the performance. I can't tell you how much better this makes shows, for audiences and comedians alike. Another thing that venues can do is put up signs and issue advance warnings about language and topics that may legitimately be too difficult for some audience members (and too triggering for fragile, thin-skinned crybabies).

As comedy consumers, there are things you can do to support the ways in which good comedy enhances people's lives. You can learn about other cultures. You can stop taking yourself so seri-ously. You can stop coddling children into adulthood—they'll be fine, and a lot more prepared to be out on their own. You can cut out the faux outrage over trivial things. You can stop judging oth-ers. You can take the time to listen and consider the source and intent of a joke instead of defaulting to knee-jerk reactions. You can think for yourself. You can trust yourself. And you can open yourself up to trusting us.

If you think Dave Chappelle's special is offensive, then don't watch it. If you think Bill Burr is abrasive, then turn him off and go bowling. Nothing good comes from silencing comedians. NOTHING. When it comes to freedom, we're canaries in the coal mine. Attacking us distracts from more important issues. Use that energy to demand a cleaner environment, law-abiding corpora-tions, transparent government, effective health policies, or safer schools and streets. Stop reacting to every little ping on your phone. Read a fucking book. And by all means, stop attacking the people whose only goal in life is to make you laugh. We're not the enemy.

I will leave you with a tweet from Ricky Gervais that, for me, puts it all into perspective: "I'd like to apologize for the joke I've just written. It is sick and unnecessary and shouldn't be said in public. Please remember I've already said sorry when you hear it. Thanks."

The most important thing of all? Laugh! Let go and laugh!

ACKNOWLEDGMENTS

Thank you to Eddie Sarfaty. I honestly don't know what I would do without your help and expertise. You took my crazy brain and made sense of it, and for that you deserve a medal. Thank you for organizing my thoughts, arguments, and ideas, so that other people could understand them. Book: $22.99. Eddie's contribution: priceless.

Thank you to Ria Dillulo, for your research, formatting, focus, perfectionism, and amazing fire-making prowess. And thanks for stretching me out.

Thank you to Lynn Grady, for finding me and asking me to write this book.

I am grateful and humbled to have the powerful Dey Street women support me. Special thanks to my editor, Alessandra Bastagli. And thank you to Carrie Thornton, Rosy Tahan, Kell Wilson, Heidi Richter, Kendra Newton, and Tatiana Dubin. What a team!

Thank you to Malaga Baldi, for your generosity, advice, cheerleading, and incessant reminders.

Thank you to Rick Dorfman, for always having my back even when you don't call me back.

Thank you to Glenn Schwartz, for always thinking out of the box, and never standing on one.

Thank you, Estee Adoram, Ted Alexandro, Larry Amoros, Ahmed Ahmed, Joy Behar, Sandra Bernhard, David Bianculli, Lewis Black, Elyane Boosler, Laurie Braun, Kelly Carlin, Margaret

Cho, Marjorie Cohen, Susie Dietz, Peter Dillulo, Noam Dworman, Susie Essman, Isabel Evans, Louis Faranda, Janeanne Garofalo, Ira Glasser, Dara Gottfried, Gilbert Gottfried, Kathy Griffin, Gary Gulman, Anabelle Gurwitz, Caroline Hirsch, Sue Hollingsworth, Amazon Jackson, Geri Jewell, Judy Katz, Eleanor Kerrigan, Laurie Kilmartin, Gary Kordan, Henriette Mantel, Friar James Martin, Michael Moynihan, Rosie O'Donnell, Nimesh Patel, the Paley Center for Media (Mark, Melani, and Patty), Luanne Peterpaul, Jill Stauffer and David LaFrance at the Provincetown Commons, Joan Rivers, Chris Rock, Howard Rosenstein, Kate Moira Ryan, Eve Sadof-Schwartz, Sam Seder, Mitzi Shore, Brittany Sowards, Jon Stewart, Court Stroud, Robin Tyler, Rob Weisbach, Suzanne Westenhoefer, Caroline Wexler, Brad Williams, Justine Ungaro, and Maysoon Zayid.

Thank you to Lucy, for keeping us company. Even though your separation anxiety destroyed my blinds, you are the best dog in the world.

Thank you to Ruth and Harold Gold, for raising me with a sense of humor, for teaching me the importance of a good work ethic, and for never underestimating the power of a good laugh.

Thank you to my incredible children, Henry and Ben, who put up with an entire year of me screaming, "Keep it down! Do you understand that I have to write a book?" I love you both more than anything. And remember that I'm counting on you to pluck my chin hairs when I'm lying in my own urine at the Hebrew Home for the Aged.

And to my beautiful Elysa, for her unwavering love and support through this process and for never asking me, "How much more do you have to write? Do you think you'll be done in time? When is this going to be over already?" (Okay, the last one might have been during sex.) I love and adore you always.

NOTES

CHAPTER 1: IT'S NOT FUNNY UNTIL THE FAT LADY CRIES

1. Derald Wing Sue et al., "Racial Microaggressions in Everyday Life: Implications for Clinical Practice," *American Psychologist* 62, no. 4 (May–June 2007): 271–86.

CHAPTER 2: SAY THAT AGAIN, AND I'LL WASH YOUR MOUTH OUT WITH SOAP

1. Eleanor Roosevelt, My Day column, October 29, 1947.

CHAPTER 5: SOMETIMES THE TRUTH HURTS

1. Ramsey Ess, "Unearthing Steve Allen and Lenny Bruce's Unaired Discussion on Free Speech," Vulture, July 27, 2012.
2. "NIGHTCLUBS: The Sickniks," *Time,* July 13, 1959; David E. Kaufman, *Jewhooing the Sixties: American Celebrity and Jewish Identity* (Waltham, MA: Brandeis University Press, 2012).

CHAPTER 7: THERE'S A REASON IT'S CALLED AN "ACT"

1. Alan Duke, "Andrew Dice Clay Is Back with 'No Apologies,'" CNN.com, December 29, 2012.
2. Donald Trump, on *CNN Tonight with Don Lemon,* aired August 8, 2015, on CNN.

CHAPTER 8: COMPARING APPLES TO ORANGE FUCKFACE PRESIDENTS

1. Meri Wallace, "Name Calling," *Psychology Today,* January 24, 2016.
2. German Lopez, "The Reagan Administration's Unbelievable Response to the HIV/AIDS Epidemic," Vox, December 1, 2016.
3. Will Rogers, Will Rogers Says column, November 23, 1932.

CHAPTER 9: DUH! WHAT DID YOU EXPECT?

1. Howard Stern, *Private Parts* (New York: Simon & Schuster, 1993).

CHAPTER 10: CAN WE TALK? PLEASE?

1. Joan Rivers, editorial, *Washington Post,* August 24, 2012.
2. Joan Rivers, on *Watch What Happens Live with Andy Cohen,* aired February 16, 2012, on Bravo.
3. THR Staff, "Toronto: Chris Rock's Emotional, Hilarious Tribute to 'Mount Rushmore' Joan Rivers," *Hollywood Reporter,* September 7, 2014.
4. Julie Miller, "Prince Charles Is Just as Broken Up over Joan Rivers's Death as We Are," *Vanity Fair,* September 4, 2014.

ABOUT THE AUTHOR

JUDY GOLD is an American stand-up comedian, actress, television writer, and producer. She won two Daytime Emmy Awards for her work as a writer and producer on *The Rosie O'Donnell Show*, and has starred in comedy specials on HBO, Comedy Central, and Logo. She has also written and starred in two critically acclaimed hit Off-Broadway shows: *The Judy Show: My Life as a Sitcom* and *25 Questions for a Jewish Mother*. She is currently the host of the hit podcast *Kill Me Now*.